EPIC FOOD FIGHT

∿Epic∿ Food Fight

a bite-sized history of SALVATION

FATHER LEO PATALINGHUG

servant

AN IMPRINT OF
FRANCISCAN MEDIA
Cincinnati, Ohio

Cover and book design by Mark Sullivan
Cover image: Hugo van der Goes (c.1440-82)
detail of *The Fall*, after 1479 (oil on panel)
Kunsthistorisches Museum, Vienna, Austria / The Bridgeman Art Library

LIBRARY OF CONGRESS CATALOGING-IN-PUBLICATION DATA
Patalinghug, Leo E.
Epic food fight : a bite-sized history of salvation / Father Leo Patalinghug.
pages cm
Includes bibliographical references and index.
ISBN 978-1-61636-664-3 (alk. paper)
1. Food—Religious aspects—Christianity. 2. Salvation—Christianity. I. Title.
BR115.N87P38 2014
230'.2—dc23
2013041321
ISBN: 978-1-61636-664-3

Published by Servant, an imprint of Franciscan Media
28 W. Liberty St.
Cincinnati, OH 45202
www.FranciscanMedia.org

DEDICATED TO

. . .

my parents and family

. . .

St. John Paul II, who used my chalice at a sacred liturgy and
encouraged me to be a good priest

. . .

to Blessed Teresa of Calcutta and her sisters as they feed the
poorest of the poor

. . .

to all of the priests and consecrated women and men;
and, to the holy people of God in my life who have fed me
body, mind, and soul.

• CONTENTS •

I would like to acknowledge all those involved in the culinary and food service world: whether you are a celebrity chef, professional chef, those in the hospitality and service industry, rectory cooks, home cooks, cafeteria workers, or soup kitchen volunteers. There are so many who have a passion to serve food with a godly love! In many of these "faithful foodies," I have silently observed a charism from God, a burning desire to create more than a meal. With their gifts, they share an experience of fellowship and a place at the table where we can celebrate the work of human hands, share love for one another, and therefore learn how to love God as the Giver of all good things.

The Appetizer

Smack! The tater tot hit me in the face. The surprise made me lose my balance. The drink on my tray spilled and splashed on my unsuspecting classmate. He was just as shocked, and I was mortified! Along with my drink, my tater tots fell onto the table. At this point, some of my fellow sophomores grabbed handfuls of them and hurled them across the cafeteria. Someone yelled, *"Food fight!"* And at that moment, food of every type and from every direction rained down, not like manna from heaven, but like bird droppings—annoying, messy, and disgusting forms of what I call "former food." That was my first food fight experience—as well as my first experience of detention. And I didn't even start it. But, in a battle, no one is completely innocent, and everyone feels the punishment.

My second food fight experience came about when I was studying at the Pontifical North American College, the American seminary in Rome, Italy. While it was certainly an incredible experience to study theology in a city imbued with spiritual lessons (and so many restaurants!), I was a bit sad to be so far from my own family. I was also a little intimidated by the prospect of living in a foreign country for so many years because, honestly, I was not fond of Italian food.

This particular food fight occurred in my heart and soul. I was tempted to be discouraged because I didn't think I would enjoy myself. My homesickness made me question the bishop's authority in sending me to Rome in the first place. My bad attitude stemmed from the fact that Italian food was so different from the earthy, briny flavors of well-marinated Filipino food—especially my family's home cooking! Would I starve? Would I fit into an all Anglo-American seminary in a country full of Italians (some of whom didn't realize that a Filipino could also actually be an American)? The interior fight continued as I questioned whether I would be able to learn anything relevant to my priesthood, especially since all of my classes were taught in the Italian language.

Even though most people would say that I'm very extroverted and outgoing, they don't realize how much work it takes for me to be a public person. The battle in my soul was truly food oriented, but it was quite subtle. Would I trust that Jesus could feed my body, mind, and soul? Did I believe that my shepherd—my archbishop—wanted to bring me to this specific pasture so that I could feed on the closeness of the Good Shepherd's vicar, namely the pope?

It was only after opening my mouth with an open mind that I found that God indeed would provide! I discovered, after facing my own frustrations and prejudice, that real Italian food is wonderfully delicious and very dissimilar to the style of so-called "Italian" food served in popular restaurants in America (which I have always disliked, and even more so today).

My seminary required students to share a family meal every

day of the school week. My sadness and longing for family eventually became a non-battle because those strangers who sat around the table eventually became my spiritual brothers. What I discovered in being led and fed by the Good Shepherd is that God knows what's best for me. I was like a kid discovering the deliciousness of vegetables after years of resistance to the good things Mom and Dad had wanted to share. This food fight—my interior fears and my temptation to withdraw from community and the world because of sadness and loneliness—was just as real, useless, messy, and painfully annoying as the food fight I hadn't started in high school—and not even funny. However, it helped me to prepare for my third food fight experience.

This third food fight has been more of a series of experiences I have had as a Roman Catholic priest. It occurs when I attempt to feed the flock with the truth of the faith. No matter how zealously and engagingly I try to present the faith, I know there are many people who just don't want to eat what I'm serving! A finicky flock, I have to patiently give them only bite-sized bits of truth. I have to work hard to sweeten the challenging words of the gospel, even just a little, in order to get them to see that while the truth may be painful and hard to swallow, it ultimately leads to Good News.

This food fight for souls is an ongoing battle—a seemingly losing battle. Let's admit it, the world (not the natural world that God made as "good," but the corrupt worldliness that includes the entertainment industry, an immoral pop culture, and hypocritical politics) does a much better job of feeding the flock with its half-truths and downright lies. And the flock just eats it up. All the while, the Catholic Church seems to be losing the battle as many members leave, either disillusioned by our scandals or hungry for something more, something different, or something exciting.

THE SIMPLE POWER OF A MEAL

As a young parish priest, I realized that so much evangelization and effective catechesis occurred while visiting with people around their dinner tables. I decided to use some of my culinary tools and the training that I learned from my family, my time in Rome, and some serious personal study in order to host supper clubs with parish families. This personal relationship between parish priest and parishioners eventually started the movement Grace Before Meals, an apostolate to bring individuals closer to God and to each other through the power of a simple meal. With the support of brother priests and the archbishop, I informally engaged the opportunity to use food to share the gospel message via a website, books with inspirational messages and recipes, videos, live presentations, radio, and a TV show. The growing awareness of this unique food movement for the faithful caught the attention of the Food Network, which eventually led to one of the most important food fights in my life.

This epic battle actually gave me an opportunity and a platform to gain the upper hand on the enemies of our faith. During a battle called *Throwdown! with Bobby Flay*, a world-famous chef challenged me to a surprise cooking competition. It may have been the first time ever, or at least the first time in quite some time, that a secular entertainment network highlighted the work of a Catholic priest. In this entertaining episode, watched by millions of people (the night the show aired, my website had almost two million unique visitors), I defeated a famous chef in a steak fajita competition.

While this was an intentionally humorous episode, it was also a serious competition. And this battle became a platform to nationally (and internationally) promote the positive message of the importance of family meals. Strengthening family relationships around the dinner table is a very basic and simple message, but one with profound sociological, psychological, and even theological implications.

In other words, I cook for people in order to bring them together. When family and friends—or even strangers—come together to celebrate a meal, they have the opportunity to say grace. And when God is invited to the dinner table, miracles happen!

Since this epic food fight, so beautifully celebrated by many different people, I've had the wonderful opportunity to share this message with a global audience. The reaction has been overwhelmingly positive, probably because of the simple but profound message, and because the joyful bite-sized way we bridge faith, food, and family applies to more than just Catholics.

STRONGER FAMILIES, BETTER FOOD

You might wonder how this all came about. I like to cook. I cook because I like to eat. I try to cook well because I like to eat well. And frankly, if I can serve up some delicious food for my family and friends, I make people happy. And, as a priest who serves up the Good News every day, my job is ultimately to bring people the happiness that comes from the theological virtues of faith, hope, and God's love.

Some people are still mystified that a priest could be so involved in the culinary world. But aren't priests involved in "food service"? As I continue to develop the theological and foundational elements of this apostolate, I'm coming to a better understanding of the reason behind the natural fascination and interest people have. Perhaps people, like sheep, are hungry. And maybe, despite all of the bad press about priests, the faithful flock still trust the priesthood as a familiar voice of a shepherd that will (we hope) lead them to verdant pastures where they can abundantly feast, rest confidently, and be fulfilled in their joys.

As a priest, not just offering the sacraments in a parish, but in the social media and entertainment industry, the Grace Before Meals message can be described in a few sound bites that help people digest the concept of a cooking show hosted by a priest:

"Stronger families, better food."

"Feeding people body, mind, and spirit."

"A family that prays grace together, stays together."

"A priest, as a 'father,' provides the daily Bread of Life."

You can probably think of a few other quips to describe why I do what I do. Oftentimes, I'll present my message while doing a live cooking demonstration. Audiences around the world find it interesting that I can cook and talk at the same time. More important, they discover that for an hour or so, they have been educated in an entertaining way. They realize that they are hungering for more!

With the desire to foster the New Evangelization, I've realized that the easiest way to reach people's hearts and minds is through their stomachs. I can generally keep a crowd's attention simply by chopping, dicing, mixing, and grilling. It's surprising because many of my audiences are so mixed—age, race, gender, and even different religions. The tempting aromas, the process of creating something out of nothing, and tips on how to create restaurant-quality food at home makes it almost easy to win them over to listen to the Good News, a message that satisfies the soul. For me, food and the fascinating cooking process is a means to an end. The cooking and the food itself leads to something far more important: a communion of persons around the common meal, around the table, and around the celebration of life.

Jesus, too, used food and faith analogies and complimentary linguistics. He described heaven as a banquet, faith the size of a mustard seed, and even called himself the "Bread of Life." We'll discuss this more in the chapters ahead.

DIGESTING THE TRUTH OF OUR FAITH

As an important side note, this book is not intended for academic purposes. It's designed to integrate a lofty sacramental theology in a pastoral way for the sake of the flock—sheep who may not have the luxury and privilege of seminary training or upper-level theology classes but who are very capable of grasping the truths of faith—and more important, digesting them!

During a presentation in the Diocese of Corpus Christi, Texas, I did a cooking demonstration and presentation on the Eucharist as the "Food for the Human Family." How fitting to do a Eucharistic teaching in a diocese named after the Eucharist—Corpus Christi, the Body of Christ. Sitting in the packed church hall was a theologian and seminary professor who taught systematic theology. He introduced himself to me afterward and told me how much he enjoyed the presentation and the food—but more important, the food for thought. He told me that he had never heard Eucharistic theology presented in such anthropologically relevant terms. He was surprised how these theological concepts presented in a bite-sized way gave him much pause for prayer, reflection, and study. Wow—cutting onions and sautéing them with a spiritual discussion even impressed a seminary professor!

This is what I hope to do for those who read this book. I don't want to bore you with theology—because theology is far from boring. Instead, I want to make sure the theology incarnates in you—that is, takes on flesh through your person, and this requires you to not just read the information here, but to savor it, chew on it, and take time to digest it. You are what you eat! Your mind, heart, and soul are capable of digesting God's Word, especially since it becomes flesh to dwell among us.

That's why each chapter contains various segments: a prayer or Scripture quote, a theological discussion, and then ideas and questions to engage ongoing reflection. I call this "chewing on the Good News"!

SALVATION HISTORY—SUPERSIZED

In this book, I present to you what I call a "theology of food." It's a unique term, I realize. Some may think that it's silly. However,

I believe that if God made food, there must be a godly logic to it. And as I continue my own research, prayer, and reflection about the food that God provides, I realize that a great battle—a universal food fight—lies ahead. The Evil One has an objective to feed us with the food that destroys the soul, while God has the food for eternal life. This is an important part of *salvation history*, a term that describes the saving acts of God throughout all of human history as recorded in Scripture, tradition, and the magisterium (the official teaching body of the Church).

Salvation history is a humongous topic—it's supernaturally "supersized"! This book will hopefully make it more manageable, or "bite-sized." Making food and difficult topics more bite-sized is an important culinary and advertising technique to help the diner (even if that person is a so-called "cafeteria Catholic") to enjoy the meal and not be overwhelmed by it.

Unlike my previous works, in this book I won't emphasize the process of cooking food. In other words, there won't be any recipes. This is because I want to keep focus on the theological treatment, while peppering the subject with culinary inspired considerations to help you relish the meaning of the meal.

My theological approach isn't meant to replace any teachings of the Church, but simply to present them differently. In a chef's world, this technique could be described as plating a "deconstructed dish." For example, I could give you a ham-and-cheese sandwich in a traditional way—two pieces of bread, ham, and cheese toasted in a pan. A deconstructed plating of the same dish might instead use Italian prosciutto wrapped around a crouton that has some cheese curds baked into it. You would get the same or similar flavors of ham and cheese, but in a different way.

This chef-inspired deconstruction provides a good teaching tool for me. What I have found helpful in teaching the faith is to have the flock—that is, congregation—look at elements of the faith individually and in an integrated way. By putting it together in a slightly different way as it applies to a person's life, the listener is able to appreciate each part of the dish and respect the process of integration, while retaining the original essence. That's my approach.

So, now that I've provided you a little appetizer of what to expect in this book, I pray that the love of God fills your soul, and that you learn not to hunger for the things that bring you harm. As you journey on, you need to eat. There are temptations along the way that will certainly whet your appetites. Be careful. Remember, you are what you eat.

In a sense, your journey to heaven is one big food fight. Thank God, Jesus Christ conquered the temptations of the forty days of fasting in the desert, and he even became the food to accompany us until we reach the feast of feasts—the Supper of the Lamb.

Bon appétit! You'll need a healthy appetite, because God wants to feed you!

Let the battle begin!

CHAPTER ONE

God's Diet Plan

And the Lord God commanded the man, saying, "You may freely eat of any tree of the garden; but of the tree of knowledge of good and evil you shall not eat, for in the day that you eat of it you shall die." (Genesis 2:16–17)

In the beginning, everything was perfect—just as God made it. But one bite—just one bite of the forbidden fruit—set the world on a trajectory toward brokenness and sin that would eventually be healed with one bite of the blessed fruit of Mary's womb. But between the two poles of forbidden fruit and the ushering in of the victorious Supper of the Lamb, all of humanity would be at the center of a cosmic battle. And the weapon of choice between these two cosmic enemies is food!

In a sense, had Adam and Eve followed God's "diet," all would have remained perfect. But the seemingly irresistible plating used by the Evil One caused Eve to partake and share the venom with her companion. The devil hurled the first attack. God responded with a punishment and a plan to bring his creation back to a land flowing with milk and honey.

Let's look at God's approach in correcting the fatal bite of Adam and Eve. His punishment (or remedy for his sickened children) would be similar to a parent who dismisses a misbehaving child from the table before dessert. God gave them what they wanted and deserved. Did Adam and Eve want to be like God? So, go out and work as hard as God did in the creation account. "Go ahead and provide for yourselves," God would say to the two as they were cast out from the original Promised Land. God would wait for their return, just like a loving mom and dad who would save a dessert for when their prodigal child returned humble and contrite.

The one deviation from God's carefully crafted meal plan did have one positive repercussion, however. The Fall initiated God's ultimate response to pick Adam and Eve back up. That's why the Easter Vigil's proclamation calls the Fall a "happy fault." And yes, it was truly Adam and Eve's fault. We can rightly blame the first crowning creations—those who were created "immaculately" in God's image and likeness, and who by their free will chose disobedience.

They were given permission to eat any fruit from any tree without consequence. By eating the forbidden fruit from the tree of knowledge, they demonstrated the worst sides of innocence: immaturity and ignorance. To use a culinary term: an innocent or undeveloped palate that cannot respect and appreciate the finer (finest) things in life.

This fall shows a very important aspect to salvation history. It showed that, even in their innocence, our first parents had a strange appetite to be God, or at least similar enough to God to be a worthy competitor to God's authority demonstrated by their self-perceived ability to feed themselves. That was the devil's temptation: "Eat this and be like the one who created you. You don't need to listen to what he says about what to eat. You can eat whatever you want, and nothing bad will happen to you."

Adam and Eve's desire for godliness was not a foreign concept for the devil. Tradition tells us that Lucifer was one of the most powerful angels in heaven. Lucifer challenged God's authority—that is, disobeyed him. Like a rebellious child who thinks they know better than Mom and Dad, Lucifer thought he knew better than God with respect to God making humanity even more impressive than the angels. It's a temptation that any of God's creations—whether human or angelic—may face.

The temptation to test God's authority and wisdom is present throughout all of salvation history. It's a difficult one to resist. We all want to break the first commandment: There is a God, and it's not you! It's a hard commandment to swallow, but it's one that God commanded Moses to force-feed to the Israelites by breaking up the false idol of the cow and making them consume it—which no doubt would have caused them great pain and, in some cases, even death. But that's what happens when we eat the lies of the devil and somehow believe we are as powerful as God.

God, however, is a loving Father and understands that his children can be easily confused with the distinction of being more *like God* than being like *a God*. In fact, God knows that all creation hungers to be more like God because he himself stamped all of creation with his own imprimatur. We all have a craving to be one with God, to be raised up to his glory. That's what God wants for us, too, but in a more ordered, well-balanced way. We just have to follow his plan. We need to follow God's diet.

Adam and Eve were easy prey for the devil—like lambs before the prowling, roaring lion, looking for someone to devour (see 1 Peter 5:8). He knew the best way to devour one's enemy was from the inside. And the only way to get inside them was to turn sin and temptation into food.

You Are What You Eat

We are what we eat—and God wants to feed us! That's not merely a theological statement. It's a biological, sociological, and psychological reality.

The devil promised that human (creature) could become God (Creator). We know the relationship between the two is meant to be one of subject and master; it's a relationship of human weakness versus God's divine perfection and power. But for the sake of fairness, Catholic theologians tell us that God also wants us to be more like him. Jesus showed us that the way to become more like God the Father was through obedience, even if it meant that, despite his innocence, Jesus would have to die on the cross, starving for companionship and humbly swallowing the insults over the injuries. We become more like God by following the sacrifice of Jesus, who willingly served his disciples at the table—even though he was the master.

The technique the devil used with Adam and Eve continues today. The devil simply made something bad look temptingly good. We choose to sin because we are somehow convinced that we, too, will look good. We somehow think that by sinning, we will look and feel better: more powerful, stronger, smarter, more attractive—that is, we become demigods! We are all tempted, like Adam and Eve, to be our own God.

Yes, the devil is a master at "plating"—presenting his dishes artistically, interestingly, and appetizingly. Unfortunately, the Church is still learning how to plate the beauty of truth in a way that makes people want to taste it, consume it, and live it. Jesus was the master of this, evidenced by the crowds he drew who were hungry to eat up every word that came from his mouth. The Church, still stuck in the inherited brokenness of Adam and Eve, has fallen behind in proactive efforts to evangelize. We do not put resources, time, talent, or treasure in the craft of plating, and as a result, we continue to suffer the loss of many souls who, like Adam and Eve, are swayed by something inherently bad that looks so good.

This Old Testament effort on the part of the devil is alive and well today. Consider how contemporary society views religion, especially Catholicism. Today many people consider religion to be outdated (i.e., spoiled food), boring (i.e., leftovers), unappealing (i.e., unseasoned), forceful (i.e., giving solid food to babies or force-feeding someone), and judgmental (i.e., moralizing from PETA and militant vegans). As a result, people are bored, uninspired, and exhausted by Christians trying to shove truth down their throats. In response, they regurgitate, unable to digest anything. They feel nauseous, and turn instead to junk food for satisfaction. That's an honest experience for the contemporary world, one that almost encourages a cafeteria Catholicism/Christianity.

The devil, still using the same cheap tricks, has made it very easy to destroy and devour lives—from the inside—simply by making the truth look stupid or gross while transforming lies into delicacies.

Adam and Eve were no different from teenage children (or immature young adults) today who are fascinated with the occult, dabbling with pagan religions. Consider how the dark and demonic now portray themselves, especially in modern versions of vampires, werewolves, and zombies: They no longer frighten people. No, instead these modern versions of demonic incarnations are now quite attractive, and even popular. Young people don't want to be like saints. They want to be like contemporary werewolves, vampires, zombies, or killing machines from video games. It's a complete bastardization of what God eventually tells his people through the teachings of Jesus Christ: "Unless you eat the flesh of the Son of man and drink his blood, you have no life in you" (John 6:53). With the devil, the words are completely reversed: "Unless I eat your flesh and drink your blood, I will have no life in me!" Or in the case of Adam and Eve, "Eat this poison and drink this venom, and you will live!"

THE DIVINE STRATEGY

God, however, does have a strategy for winning this battle, and he also uses food as his weapon. Adam will now have to till the ground and collaborate with God's natural world in order to feed himself and provide for his family. In liturgical language, he will have to develop the fruit of the earth through the work of human hands in order to eventually eat the Bread of Life. On Adam rests a great responsibility, a reminder of sorts that his job was to feed his wife. Had he done a better job of fulfilling his wife's craving, Eve would have not been tempted to go elsewhere to be fed. (We'll discuss this more thoroughly in chapter five).

Eve's punishment will be the pains of birth—in particular, a type of morning sickness that comes when the mother's biology adjusts to feeding a child in her womb and experiences the pain of sleepless nights due to having to feed her child from her own flesh and blood. What God did for us, we now have to do for ourselves. Adam and Eve deserved this "punishment" as a remedy for their deadly choice in sharing a meal with the Evil One. As a result, inheriting the brokenness and the consequences of the Fall, the rest of humanity now worries between paychecks and struggles to provide the daily bread for themselves and their children. In a sense, the remedial punishment to till the ground and experience the pains of childbearing—something God did not want us to have to do—is now a part of our everyday life. However, there is a purpose to it all.

The devil also experienced a severe punishment, which is the same for all unrepentant prodigal children: to live with the irrational hunger for power. The devil has been so consumed by arrogance that he will never be able accept the reality of simply being a very limited creature (albeit an angelic one). The devil will have to forever live with the craving for something that can never be: being the one true God! What a punishment! The devil desperately wanted to be the food for Adam and Eve; he wanted to be the one who fed them. The devil hungers for this power, but he will never have it. The devil will see the true food—the only way to become more like God—but will always refuse to eat it. That is truly a perfect punishment for the Antichrist.

This same pain consumes people every day who work so hard that they neglect to spend time with their families, somehow thinking that overwork will help them feel like they are the true providers for the family. They forget that there are many families who, although they have much fewer material possessions, are happier because they spend time with each other.

The deep significance regarding food in the first few pages of sacred Scripture indicates a theology of food on a very human level. God is concerned with feeding his people. As a father provides for children, so God wants to provide for us, because he is truly our Father. We however, turn away from the meal, and instead crave junk food that causes lethargy, brokenness, sickness, and eventually death. Throughout the Old Testament, God reveals his desire to feed us and show us how we become more like him when we in turn feed others. However, when we think we can feed ourselves and make that the priority rather than feeding others (as God does), we fall back into the same eating disorder that the devil caused from that first bite.

Food Fights in the Desert

The food fight continues in the desert—the decisive battleground where the chosen people would have to live after the Exodus from the slavery of the Egyptians. In this desert, which Christ will eventually redeem in his own salvific battle, the people will experience the food fight in severe and miraculous ways. Consider how food becomes the driving force used by God to bring about salvation in the history of the chosen people.

The Exodus and Passing Over the Food Enslavement (Exodus 11). The Jewish people grumbled against Moses, the prophetic leader who was guiding them to the Promised Land flowing with milk and honey. In their stubborn hungers, the Israelites recalled how well they ate when they were slaves. In their sickness, they would rather return to slavery just so they could eat free food, even if they were slaves! Instead of working to improve their situation, they depended on a false master that enslaved them by psychologically and spiritually turning their stomachs and their cravings into a god.

The Provisions of Manna, Meat, and Rock-Hard Water (Exodus 16). Moses interceded and God provided a unique foreshadowing of the heavenly bread. The people complained again and again, craving meat. God, annoyed by their lack of trust and their lack of gratitude for the food given to them, did rain down food in the measure of their complaint—to the point that the food was coming out of their nostrils. Their complaints resulted in the sickness and death that comes from the experience of gluttony—one of the deadly sins. God had instructed Moses to use his staff to split the Red Sea, and that same staff would now be used in anger to split the rock that poured forth water. These unique desert meals showed the struggle between humility and arrogance, between Crock-Pot patience and angry experiences of fast-food drive-in patrons, and between the wonder of God's providence to provide manna and humanity's need to sample something mysterious, foreign, and new.

The Return of the Snakes (Numbers 21:8). As the Israelites' grumbling stomachs turned into complaints that took root in their hearts, God once again revealed how ugly the people appeared and how their nagging sounded to him. God showed them how they had become like "snakes" intent on poisoning others through their grumbling, doubt, gossip, and rebellion against authority. The seraph serpents seemingly win the battle by eating into the flesh of the people. When the people face the ugly truth by looking at the serpent lifted on the pole, they would be healed. This, we already know, is the prefigured image of the ugliness manifested in the scandal of the crucified body of Jesus. What heals the Israelites is the venom of truth—the ability to look at what they have become. It was difficult to digest, but simply looking bravely at the exalted truth—in this case the ugly image of the serpent that they as a people began to resemble—healed them. And humility is one of the toughest pills to swallow.

Deuteronomy's Mandate to Celebrate (Deuteronomy 16). With a very specific plan, God instructed Moses to initiate feast days. The first commandment, to love God above all things, is a mandate for celebration. Specifically, the People of the Covenant are called to commemorate the Passover in the month of *Abib* by eating the unleavened bread. They are called to count the Feast of Weeks by the farming cycle of the sickle cutting down the standing grain, and the Feast of Booths to make an offering—a generous offering—for the blessings God has given to them. The Jewish cycle of celebrations and the calendar of every monotheistic religion (Christianity, Islam) share a cyclical pattern of commemorating God with a celebration that involves food. These feast days require that we either eat something to remember God, or fast (or not eat some things) to remember we are *not* God! Either way, God uses, instructs, and mandates a balanced cycle of feasting to strengthen his family.

A Lasting Sip and Bite (1 Kings 17). Prophets helped expound God's desire to provide for his children. And, when God's people provide the same service—that is, when they feed those in need before they feed themselves (as a loving parent does), that person becomes what they crave most: They become more like God. Consider the case of the widow of Zarephath and her son. When Elijah asked the widow to provide him with a cup of water and a small cake, she took a big risk— a leap of faith if you will— and used the only remaining flour and oil to make a cake for a stranger. Because she did, God blessed these unselfish souls. He miraculously provided for them!

Joseph's "Well-Fared" Program (Genesis 37). The humility Joseph exhibited by serving the brothers who once left him to be food for wild beasts shows the image of a man trying to follow God's diet. The number of droughts and crop-destroying plagues in the Old Testament are significant reminders that God used food (or its lack) to humble his people. Joseph's willingness to provide food for his brothers who jealously abandoned him combats the arrogant disobedience of their ancestors, and it brought God's people back on the path to a history that saves— not destroys.

A Kingly Craving (2 Samuel 11). David, the Jewish people's king of kingdoms, reveals the battle between God's goodness and the devil's evil, and how the conniving one-bite lingers in the hearts of even exalted people. While David, evidently infused with inspired virtue, still possessed the concupiscence that convinces him to lure Uriah with fatty foods and overindulgence in drink as a way to kill him. He is the husband of Bathsheba, the woman David lusted after—that is, unhealthily craved. When David accepts the bitter pill of truth about his actions through the words of the prophet Nathan, he exercises the tenets of his faith through fasting until he reaches a restored health. And only when he's healthy enough (spiritually) does he end that period of mourning by feasting.

The Prophet Preparing Us for the Feast from Heaven (Isaiah 7). Isaiah's prophecy brings to light a unique perspective of this Promised Land flowing with "milk and honey." It starts with Isaiah chapter 7, when we hear about how God has been preparing Israel for a "Feast of Feasts," beginning with a "sign"—namely, that a virgin shall conceive and bear a son. Christians hearing those words will automatically think of the season of Advent and the feast of Christmas. But through that prophetic voice, God uses Isaiah to show how he will call people back to that place of peace—a holy mountain where weapons like swords and spears are transformed into pruning hooks and sickles for harvesting.

Dieting Until Death (2 Maccabees 7:20). Finally, I'd like to consider how following God's diet leads his people to become true witnesses of faith. The seven sons of a widow resisted eating the forbidden food (swine's flesh) at the irreligious order of the pagan king. These seven brothers had to decide whether to defile their bodies with forbidden food or have their bodies torn apart by the order of the king. The heroic mother's encouragement, watching each son die, speaks of God's mercy given to those who never forsake his laws. This faithful family demonstrated more than obedience to a physical teaching. They wanted to be spiritually obedient, not just physically healthy. They wanted to eat what God wanted them to eat, not what their lower appetites may have craved or what the authorities may be forcing them to eat out of fear. In other words, they wanted to savor their faith and be free from the renewed temptations of the devil or the persecution of ungodly people. They refused to eat the foods that their religion proscribed as unclean. Theologically, food became the source of the battle between life and death. If they ate the forbidden foods, they would live physically but die spiritually. If they refused to eat the food, they would be subject to a gruesome death. But God would end their ordeal with a glorious feast—in heaven.

Food, again and again! It initiated salvation history, and through the patriarchs, prophets, judges, and kings, food has been used to sustain salvation history. Food helped the People of the Covenant to remember that God wants to feed us—as a true shepherd's desire to feed the flock. If the shepherd does not feed the flock, the sheep will wander and certainly be lost looking for food. A lost sheep will become an easy meal for the wolf, the serpent, and ultimately the apocalyptic dragon!

FOOD FOR THOUGHT

It seems that almost every other page in the Old Testament references people celebrating a covenant with food, breaking a covenant through gluttony or getting drunk, or using food to pay off a debt or stop a war. It is not my objective in this book to analyze each passage of the Scriptures that references food. That's the daunting task of biblical scholars, those who are dedicated to chewing, digesting, savoring, and feeding the flock with God's Word. It's no doubt a challenging task to reveal the nuances and impact of Scripture, in the same way a sommelier strives to help wine lovers to discern and appreciate (so not to abuse) a sip of the finest of Canaan's wine. However, in this cursory look at the Old Testament, as God's people we also have a responsibility to be schooled in the Bible, even though most of us will never become official scholars.

Marcion of Sinope, a bishop in the second century, believed that Old Testament was inferior, or unequal, to the New Testament. Unfortunately, contemporary society has its share of Marcionic tendencies. In our modern mentality, most of us don't spend too much time in prayer, study, and meditation of the Old Testament. As such, our understanding of salvation history is often skewed and immature. My objective is simply to provide a systematic theology of food that comes *before* a systematic demonstration of the theology of the Eucharist as food.

To speak even more plainly, the reason why Christians—and

many Catholics, too—do not understand the sacrament of the Eucharist as God's Sacred Feast is because they haven't been well evangelized in the sacramental activity of the family meal. A careful reading of the Hebrew Scriptures through a hermeneutic (or study) of food prepares us for a loftier and more spiritual understanding of the food given to us in the New Testament, namely the Eucharist. But before people can be catechized well about that mystery of faith, they must first be evangelized about the commonsense teaching of what food means to us as humans. A theology of food, as a precursor to a Eucharistic theology, considers the anthropological, sociological, biological, and psychological connections of food and faith.

In the Fullness of Time

From the beginning of creation, God gave us light to see his Trinitarian communion revealed in stages of salvation history, and these stages necessarily involved food. Because of our limited human minds and fickle appetites, God gave bite-sized glimpses of his ultimate plan to defeat the Evil One, who desires to feed God's children with a corrupt diet that ultimately leads to death.

And while God the providential Father could force-feed us "supernaturally," he also knows that a supernatural longing for heavenly food can come when we develop a natural longing and hunger for good and healthy food in general. It seems that God continued the unfolding events of salvation history to encourage a hunger in his children. Between now and the time we arrive at that heavenly banquet, we must struggle with the smorgasbord of choices that are set before us. God provides, but the devil also offers some horrible options, albeit attractively presented. Adding to the confusion, agnostics, atheists, politicians, entertainment moguls, capitalists, and—worst of all—relativists all chime in, all of them vying for the attention of an already confused flock of easily persuaded followers. Like shoppers in a mall taking free samples from restaurant employees, we (the sheep) wander from pasture to pasture, nibbling here, there, and everywhere, ultimately destroying our appetite for God's true food.

To complicate matters, God gives us the gift of freedom to choose where we want to eat. Freedom is God's gift to his children. Freedom describes God, and as such, God's children should also be free. God won't force-feed us. He wants us to choose the true food on our own. And when we do, we become what we eat—we become more like God, who is free.

As a part of God's plan to feed his children, he will himself "when the time [has] fully come" (Galatians 4:4), return from heaven as a lamb to show how following God's diet will lead to more than a healthy life: It will lead to eternal life!

At this moment in salvation history, God stops the continuum and redirects us back to the original plan, the Garden of Eden. This garden, filled with the goodness of a perfect land, flowed with milk and honey. It was a place where creatures did not worry about what they would eat because God himself would feed them.

In this U-turn at "the fullness of time," the New Adam (Jesus) will now come from the New Eve (Mary), and this New Eve will be responsible for feeding the New Adam. We need to view all of salvation history as though we were looking in a mirror. We see the truth as the exact opposite of what we believe it to be. We also see the destination (the Garden of Eden), but we get there, in a sense, by walking "backward" to it. But, our walk backward is not walking blindly, because the mirror of faith shows us where to go—with a unique perspective. The historical experiences of God's people—which we are reminded of each Passover feast—should better inform us so that the food we decide to consume and make a part of our pilgrimage will aid us, not hurt us.

God uses that U-turn moment to give us an obedient Eve (*Eva* in Latin), who will be greeted with an "Ave"—which means "hail." Salvation history's victory for God begins with the mirror image of the New Eva obediently offering to follow God's plan, unlike the first Eva's disobedience. The New Eve will also conceive the Blessed Fruit in her womb that, in the fullness of time, will hang ripe from the Tree of Life for all to eat and drink. This Blessed Fruit from the Tree of Life will be God's ultimate weapon to reverse the destructive tendency that comes from the poison of the forbidden fruit from the Tree of Knowledge.

The New Testament, beginning with the Incarnation of Jesus Christ in Mary's womb, invites the flock to now walk backward toward the feast of the Garden of Eden. With more mature faith and matured knowledge, we walk by faith (not by sight), but the Mirror of Justice[1] carefully helps us to maneuver through life back to that Garden, carefully and freely choosing what food we will eat along the way.

Something to Chew On

Create a menu from the Old Testament based on the ingredients that the Jewish people craved or the food that God gave to his people through Moses. When making the meal, seek out some of the traditional ways that these ingredients are used. Take the opportunity, as you cook for family or friends, to commemorate this meal as part of the covenant you want to make with them. For example, cook this meal as an anniversary dish for your spouse, or create a menu specifically for one of your children to be prepared annually on his or her birthday, or simply make a dish to celebrate a happy moment for your best friend.

Use ingredients like leeks, garlic, unleavened bread, bitter herbs, or even poultry like quail to make this a special meal.

Practical Theology for the Dinner Table

1. How do you explain the "forbidden fruit" to your children and others entrusted to your care?
2. What are some forbidden fruits in your life?
3. What feast day helps you remember that God's providence wants to feed you?
4. What is the most scriptural meal that you have made?
5. What is the one food or thing that can easily enslave you? Or, what has been the way the devil has tempted you to take a bite of something that looked good but in hindsight was harmful to your soul?

• CHAPTER TWO •

The Truth Becomes Flesh to Feed the World

Lifting up his eyes, then, and seeing that a multitude was coming to him, Jesus said to Phillip, "How are we to buy bread, so that these people may eat?" This he said to test him, for he himself knew what he would do. (John 6:5)

*F*rom the beginning of creation, God revealed his creative purpose: to feed us. It's simple but profound. Just consider the technicalities that go into feeding a newborn, or a child with an eating disorder, a finicky teenager, a young adult on a diet, a bedridden person able to eat only through a tube, or a someone approaching the last days of life. Deepening our understanding of God's objective to feed us reveals a new initiative in the heart of God, but one planned from all eternity. No longer will humanity simply be fed with earthly food; God wants to feed his people with something substantially different, new and eternal.

What God wants to feed his people is part of Jesus's plan in the New Testament. Recall how the Old Testament is filled with images of unleavened bread, heavenly manna, milk and honey, bitter herbs, and even drinking the tears of sorrow from the chalice of contrition. All of this establishes a relationship of trust and develops an understanding of God as a providential Father. The Old Testament shows how God fulfills his covenant: He provides! Yet, his chosen people still looked elsewhere, like fickle sheep, to be fed with the seeds of destruction in just one bite.

Salvation history shows that feeding God's people required more than food miraculously appearing in the desert. It required God coming to earth in order to feed us with a particular food: himself!

THE MYSTERY OF THE INCARNATION

If we understand the New Testament as the fulfillment of the Old Testament, the "theory" of God wanting to feed his people becomes a more tangible reality. Christianity calls this the mystery of the Incarnation: God coming in the flesh and blood of Jesus Christ to become food and drink for us.

This incarnate idea of God feeding us with his own flesh and blood is known as the "sacramental theology of the Eucharist," and it has been taught systematically as part of the Church's salvation history. However, before this lofty teaching can be absorbed, Jesus developed a theology of food in a more anthropological way—and with a divine twist. After all, Jesus is God. His teaching of the sacred Jewish Scripture was more than just stories of old. In Jesus's revelation, these Old Testament teachings point to something that is becoming new again, perfectly new, in his person.

The Church's deep sacramental theology of the Eucharist is built on Jesus's understanding of food for the sake of food— that is, to satisfy hunger. Jesus reveals a deeper meaning of food because he wants to satisfy a deeper sense of hunger. The grumblings of the Jewish people in the desert and the dietary laws were merely human indicators of a deeper hunger. God provided that human sustenance, not discounting its importance, but showing that the physical eating of food for the "belly" demonstrates his desire to address human hunger and care for the body, which will one day be resurrected in perfection. While many people limit God to a spiritual comfort and care, Jesus tells us that God also cares about our bodies, especially since we are part of the Body of Christ. The systematic theology of the Eucharist points to a deeper reality. But food *per se* (i.e., in and of itself) is also a profound mystery worth pondering through a theological lens. We can start by investigating how Jesus approached food, beginning with the moment he entered this world: as a cluster of cells in his mother's womb.

The Feast of the Incarnation, now celebrated in the Roman calendar nine months prior to Christmas, demonstrates the unique relationship between Jesus and food. Jesus became dependent on Mary to feed him. His first moment on earth, paralleled with his last moments on the cross, thirsting for drink, demonstrated a vulnerability—a hunger and thirst. In silence, out of a maternal love, Jesus would need to be fed in his mother's womb. In silent agony, with his mother and beloved disciple looking on helplessly, he would thirst for souls.

An Indelible Mark

One day as I meditated on the crucifix, my gaze stopped on Jesus's belly button. I know most people focus on his physical wounds. But as I tried to see more deeply the interior pain of his heart, I was directed to the statue of Mary, standing nearby and pointing to the cross. Her fingertip actually pointed to his belly button. He had one! Now it probably happened that the placement of the statue was lower than originally intended, but it gave me great pause to consider that Mary's first physical connection to Christ was just that: his belly button!

My meditation, odd as it may have been, revealed to me that I had something in common with Jesus. My prayer taught me, that the belly button is, in a sense, an "indelible mark," an irremovable sign that Jesus knew what it was like to be hungry—not just as a supernatural battle with the devil in the desert for forty days, but as a normal, everyday, human experience. From the moment he was conceived in his mother's womb, Jesus had an instant connection to food. The Almighty God made himself vulnerable to feel hunger. The Incarnation shows a human characteristic that would be with him in his last dying moments: "I thirst" (John 19:28).

Jesus's humanity and his biological need to be fed himself gives power and personal force to his teaching that when we feed the hungry and give drink to the thirsty, we do to it to him (see Matthew 25:31–46).

From an interreligious interpretation, the fact that God would allow himself to feel hungry makes some Muslims and Jews very uncomfortable. They believe that if God becomes man, vulnerable to the things we broken humans experience, he becomes *less* of a God. For Christians, however, the Incarnation of God—including Jesus's vulnerability—shows the unique character of God's omni-benevolence through the virtue of compassion and the responsibility of companionship.

COMPASSION AND COMPANIONSHIP

Theologically and etymologically, *compassion* describes God's free choice *to suffer with* his people. The root word, *cum passio* means to suffer (*passio*) with (*cum*). What makes Jesus such a loving God is that he doesn't view our suffering from afar. He views it close up; he experiences it himself. While cynics believe that vulnerability is a sign of weakness, this Christological compassion has always proven to be a unique form of strength. It's one of the weapons God uses to defeat the devil in the fight for a person's soul. The fact that Jesus, as the Lord of Lords, has compassion and is willing to suffer with his people makes him the most credible leader. He leads by example. His compassion draws people to his cause, which is ultimately to love one another as God loves us—perfecting the Golden Rule, which requires us to feed even those who cannot repay us (see John 13:34).

At the same time, Christ's vulnerability to experience hunger demonstrates a theological understanding of *companionship*. On a human level, this is the most obvious food and faith connection that Jesus tries to make. We understand companionship as walking with someone on a journey, but it is more than that! It's the combination of the two Latin words: *cum*, meaning *with*, and *pane* meaning *bread*. By virtue of Jesus's incarnation and his free choice to become vulnerable, Jesus seeks to become a companion, someone with whom to break bread on the journey. We see this when Jesus appeared to the two walking on the road to Emmaus. These men, walking together, talking about faith, discovered the object of their faith—Jesus—in the breaking of the bread. Jesus became their companion in every sense of the word. Food accompanied these men on their Emmaus walk and also became part of salvation history.

Revelation about God's desire to be compassionate and to be a companion with his people is beautifully summarized in the book of Revelation. While some people fear that book, those who want to participate more fully in salvation history are comforted by the fact that Jesus wants to walk with us in our suffering and wants to break bread to give us strength on our way. The Church's sacrament of viaticum describes Revelation's approach to food. "Behold, I stand at the door and knock; if anyone hears my voice and opens the door, I will come in to him and eat with him, and he with me" (Revelation 3:20). God chooses to feed us in a more familiar and intimate way. He wants to share more than the cup of sorrows. He seeks to break bread— something Jesus did over and over again, to the point of making it a sacramental rite in Holy Communion and also in viaticum, the last sacrament received by the faithful. Jesus wants to go *via*, "on the way"—*ti cum*, "with you." He himself is the food for our pilgrimage to heaven. He is the food that gives us everlasting life.

History has shown that, far from being a negative sign of weakness, God's desire to experience vulnerability (i.e., compassion) and his desire to eat with common sinners (i.e., companionship) is a sign of strong, virtuous character. Consider how world leaders prove their strength by example, or how people of fame, whether politicians or celebrities, gain credibility whenever they are seen doing what common folk do. Consider how much more respect, admiration, devotion, and love is gained when someone of greatness has dinner with the simple, or when the rich and famous do something humble, such as feeding the poor. That's why politicians relish the photo opportunities of eating at a county fair or attending a local barbecue. They want to demonstrate that they are on the same level as the people they seek to lead.

Such humble leadership is seen in the Incarnation. In the Word becoming flesh, we see heavenly compassion and companionship in the flesh and blood of Christ. These godly attributes become weapons in God's hand and hasten the victory over the arrogance of the devil in the epic battle for souls. The devil does not want to eat with us, or break bread with us. The devil wants to devour us by giving us a poisonous bite and leaving us to die in our destructive food choice.

The natural desire for God to feed his people is merely a precursor—an *appetizer*, if you will—to the loftier and most sacred form of food: the heavenly feast. But before we get to heaven for this feast, we must learn how to find Jesus in the companionship that occurs when two or three are gathered in his name and break bread together.

THE BASICS OF BREAD

Jesus's birth in Bethlehem carries great theological significance. The City of David, Bethlehem, establishes a connection to the

Davidic throne through Jesus's foster father, Joseph. Without the connection through Joseph as part of the Davidic heritage, Jesus's kingship would be denied, or at least theologically disputed. However, the town of Bethlehem also provides a framework for Jesus's unique approach to food, and introduces God's desire to feed his children with the "Bread of Life" (see John 6:35). The town of Bethlehem has etymological origins meaning the "House of Bread."

The city's significance hearkens to David's kingly approach in winning people over by simply providing bread (see 2 Samuel 6:19). God chose to reveal himself in the process of bread making, which requires the combination of crushed wheat, oil, salt, leaven, water, and fire—all images with great theological significance. Making bread is not only scientific; it's miraculous! Before we can grasp the deeper sacramental theology, we need to discover, appreciate, and integrate a theological anthropology of food into our more pious approach to the Eucharist.

Salvation history as revealed in the New Testament shows how Jesus, as the bread come down from heaven, was placed in a manger. The word *manger* has deep food references, as it's known as a feeding trough for animals. It shares the same roots to the Latin-influenced Italian word, *mangiare*; that is, "to eat." Already, before Jesus can even utter his first words, profound connections to food are established. He is a "foodie" from his first moments on earth.

The first witnesses of this miraculous birth, the humble shepherds, are also important to the food-centric Christological message of the New Testament. Shepherds feed their flocks.

Their pastoral attention and care reflects the promise, *"Pastores Dabo Vobis!"* God promised to give his people shepherds (see Jeremiah 3:15). This shows that from the start of Jesus's life on earth, images of food and providing shepherds will be part of God's plan to save and protect his children—the flock that continues to wander in the spiritual desert.

Furthermore, the shepherd's work—leading the flock to calm waters and verdant pastures, calling the lambs with a familiar (i.e., loving and fatherly) voice—is a concrete image of God's direct involvement in feeding his children. If the shepherd does not do his job by caring for the lambs as his own, he runs the great risk of allowing them to wander, get lost, fall into danger, and worst of all—become food for the rapacious wolves! More will be said about the shepherding qualities of Christ and his future priests in the coming chapter on the priesthood. But for now, it's important to consider the significance of this pastoral scene in which God chooses to reveal himself.

THE SILENT WORK OF LEAVEN

After the Annunciation and birth narratives, the New Testament takes on a unique silence about Jesus's life, known as the "hidden life of Jesus." While mystery surrounds the type of existence the Holy Family had from the Presentation in the Temple to the Finding of Jesus in the Temple, this hidden life of Christ involved the simple, day-to-day tasks of a family—albeit a Holy Family—doing what families needed to do to survive. They worked, played, rested on the Sabbath, celebrated the Passover meal, and lived as any other family at that time. They struggled, no doubt, with Herod's threats and the international and inter-cultural traveling Joseph had to undertake in order to protect his family's holiness. Yet, a priority for both Joseph and Mary was to make sure their child was well fed, allowing him to grow in strength and grace in the sight of God and man.

Pious tradition shows the Holy Family resting in the midst of their journeys with Joseph working with wood in the background, Mary breastfeeding Jesus while he is sleeping in her arms. Joseph was certainly a professional carpenter, but he shared the same concerns of most working fathers in that he had to provide for this very unique child! So, although these hidden years are somewhat mysterious, the common experience of family meals that shaped Jesus's humanity and human knowledge of God's mysteries became an opportunity for the family to grow in virtue. The Scriptures clearly say that Jesus grew in wisdom and strength in his daily life, most likely through his parents' faithful celebration with each other around their liturgical and family meals.

Surviving on the Word of God in God's House

The New Testament infancy narrative concludes with a unique episode, popularly known as the Finding of Jesus in the Temple. The food references, though only implied, are quite profound when we consider them.

Mary and Joseph make their annual festival pilgrimage to the Temple, this time with Jesus when he was about twelve years old. While in the caravan on their way home, Mary and Joseph realize that their son was missing. For three days, worrying, hardly eating and hardly sleeping, they find the Christ child teaching in the Temple. Finally!

Mary and Joseph were frustrated and at the same time overjoyed, but Jesus takes away all of their fears. He was healthy. He had eaten. He had slept and was safe. Who had cared for him? Could it have been the Temple Priests who sat in wonder at his knowledge? No. In fact, Jesus more accurately explains that God, his Father provided, cared for, and protected him. "How is it that you sought me? Did you not know that I must be in my Father's house?" (Luke 2:49). Jesus will say the same thing to his disciples in the presence of the Samaritan woman when he tells them that he has food that no one knows about—a secret stash that comes directly from God the Father (see John 4:32).

While his parents were naturally concerned for the human needs of Jesus, God provided something that sustained both his humanity and divinity. Doing God's will is the food that sustained Jesus. Jesus later invites all humanity to consider that we do not survive on "bread alone" (Matthew 4:4). This echoes salvation history's battle cry: God will provide! *Trust* becomes another weapon, along with *compassion* and *companionship* in achieving victory in salvation history.

AN AWKWARD FOOD MOMENT AVERTED

To continue a New Testament view of food and how it relates to the unfolding of God's plan to save humankind, Jesus begins his public ministry at a wedding banquet, prefiguring how his mission will also be fulfilled at an eternal wedding banquet (see John 2:1–11).

At this wedding, food—in particular wine—becomes the instrument of grace that initiates Mary's maternal instinct to provide the wine that comes from the fruit of her womb. She is confident that Jesus is the one who provides. At this opening of his public ministry, Mary—the New Eve—speaks her last recorded words in the Scripture. She speaks as a maidservant of the Lord to the other servants: "Do whatever he tells you." Her obedience, counteracting and counterbalancing Eve's disobedience, brings forth a sense of obedient faith in order to experience miracles. Obedience to the hunger and thirst of the wedding couple and their guests creates an opportunity for the miracle of changing water into wine—a miracle of great quality and quantity. The water used was meant for washing dishes or washing the guests' feet. The ordinariness of the elements (water) in Jesus's hands becomes something so much more—the best wine, and a lot of it!

Even the headwaiter experienced something new about this supernaturally made beverage. Normally, the economically minded newlyweds would first impress the guests with good and potent wine, getting them sufficiently inebriated so that drinking the cheaper wine later became irrelevant. At this Canaan wedding, the more expensive wine did its job. The people were already more cheerful. Now, though, with the "best wine," the guests were even more impressed with the "generosity" of the couple. The newlyweds were no doubt just as surprised. But due to Mary's humble silence, as well as the humility of the obedient servants, the source of the best wine was kept a secret. However, the observant disciples recognized that what Christ provided incomparably superseded in quality and quantity anything else they had ever experienced. That's why they began to believe in Jesus as someone extraordinary.

Jesus's approach to feeding people is generous and perfect. Jesus is not cheap. When Jesus feeds his people, he gives generously *and* he gives the very best, without cost. It's all free! Generosity in quality and quantity is an important addition to the growing list of food qualities that affect salvation history. It's exactly what the devil is not. The devil gives nothing, and when the devil makes an offer, it's never anything good.

The selfishness of the devil's trick on Adam and Eve is now reversed by the generosity of Mary and Jesus. The devil's cheap trick of making something bad (forbidden fruit) look good (delicious), only to have a bad effect (sadness and pain), is also reversed. Jesus takes something bad, or at least something common (water for cleansing), and turns it into something good (the best of wine) in order to create a good effect (a more joyful and lasting celebration). This food miracle, Christ's first, sparked wonder and amazement. It convinced the twelve disciples to become more than students. It changed their hearts to become Christ's followers, seeing him as truly the life of the celebration.

THE FEAR OF THE FISHERMAN

The second recorded miracle in Scripture, the multiplication of the loaves and fishes, had a similar effect on those who feasted on it. However, this miracle, which was witnessed by five thousand men (not counting women and children), put Jesus's culinary abilities on a global level. This miracle convinced the people of his day that they ought to proclaim Jesus king. They were still looking for a leader, the incarnate Moses and David and the prophets, who would feed them. Jesus did just that. He fed them, and they believed.

As a side note, I'd like to point out that the "five thousand men, not counting women and children" was not a sexist statement, a result of a patriarchal society. It indicated the type of responsibility a male had, as a father, to provide for his family. As the breadwinner, he collaborated with the mother's natural ability to feed people. As part of the effects of original sin, the father would have to toil and, at times, worry and pray that somehow he would have the ability to provide for his family. It's worth noting that Jesus answered the prayers of these five thousand men. As the spiritual heads of their households, they took a great risk in bringing their families on a retreat that lasted three days. Wouldn't it be wonderful if modern dads would bring their families to get to know Jesus and be fed by him?

This miracle renews salvation history's call for generosity and trust. Remember, Jesus's future priests (i.e., the first twelve seminarians in world history) failed Jesus's first pop quiz. While Jesus knew all along what he would do, he asked the disciples, "How will I feed these people?" In their worldly thinking and immature faith, they overlooked God's providence. They felt that "no one" could feed all these people. However, a possibly frightened but willing young lad's "fish sandwiches" in the hands of the One who provides became the miracle that reclaimed God's generosity in quality and quantity! The boy's generosity to share his small and simple meal was, in a sense, another miracle. Obviously, Jesus's power to multiply food in great numbers was manifested because this young lad's faith in Jesus was also great. As Jesus would later say, faith, even the size of a mustard seed, can yield even greater miracles (see Matthew 17:20).

INTENTIONAL DINNER DATES AND DIVINE DISCUSSIONS

Jesus revealed more about his Father's plan for salvation while eating and drinking with sinners. The third luminous mystery of the rosary, the Proclamation of the Kingdom and the Call to Conversion, has a special connection to Jesus's pastoral approach to ministry. He intentionally put himself in situations that would initiate great discussions and provide teaching opportunities around the dinner table. The Gospels present Jesus's Eucharistic theology in such a humanly acceptable way. He went from village to village, welcomed invitations to dine, and even—when necessary—invited himself into the homes of those who were humble and lowly, including those who were not worthy to have this honored guest under their roofs. But he said the word *ephatha* ("be opened"), and they were made worthy, healed enough to have him as their guest. Consider these food-centric dinner companions:

Zacchaeus. This tax collector literally went out on a limb to see Jesus pass by. Jesus saw how this man, known as a greedy tax collector, was silently and obscurely "reaching out" to Jesus. Jesus recognized an "open heart" and an "open door," and he used this moment to admonish Zacchaeus's judgers. Jesus entered Zacchaeus's house, and this once-greedy man would make recompense and feed the hungry.

The Repentant Women. Tradition portrays Mary Magdalene as the former prostitute who abandoned everything and followed Jesus. While often confused with the woman who washed Jesus's feet with her tears and dried them with her hair, this woman's character speaks about those on the fringe of society whom Jesus sought out as dinner companions. With these public sinners, he shared truth through parables, explained the love of the Father, and ultimately became the most expert and sweet dinner companion—something these sinners had probably not experienced in a while. Most of them probably ate alone quite often. They were unwanted and uninvited. To these, who never knew a fine dining experience, Jesus provided some of the most profound lessons of God's love.

Food Snobs. Jesus ate with the supposedly righteous as well— the leading scribes, lawyers, and Pharisees. Unfortunately, these dinner companions were more interested in breaking Jesus's growing reputation than breaking bread with him. These dinner discussions were often filled with contempt, jealousy, and legal trickery. Dinners were conniving opportunities to feed Jesus in order to trap him—like a hunter placing food in a lair. Christ used these dinner discussions to demonstrate his superior knowledge of the law. He in turn fed his guests a dose of the bitter herbs of truth. Notice Jesus's demeanor at these dinner discussions. He would enter into the battle, parrying their accusatory and condemnatory words with parables about mercy, followed with a remark about their own condemnation, and ultimately a judgment that would silence all talk. Jesus once again became the most sought-out dinner companion, because people wanted to use him—either to gain status with others by showing off that Jesus was at their home, or to trap him. The food served at these meals by those who wanted to trap Jesus became a weapon! On the other hand, Jesus used food moments to intoxicate people and help them better understand God's love.

FROM SICKNESS TO SERVANT

Jesus healed many sick people, even raising some from the dead. Food references followed these miraculous accounts. For example, the young girl who was thought to be dead would rise, and Jesus's first words were, "Give her something to eat" (see Mark 5:35–43). When Simon Peter's mother-in-law was sick with a fever, Jesus's touch healed her in such a way that she immediately became his servant and fed him (see Matthew 8:14). Although people wanted to offer Jesus hospitality, Jesus wanted to become their hospital. The indication of food, so closely related to healing and raising people from the dead, shows that Christ used food as part of the healing and life-saving process. For Jesus, food and healing went hand in hand.

A GODLY PERSPECTIVE ON FOOD

The New Testament accounts of Jesus's intimate involvement with and usage of food provide the framework for a food theology. Before understanding the Eucharist, we first need a godly perspective on food in the hands of the One who will eventually become the food of eternal life. Parables of faith the size of a "mustard seed" (Matthew 17:20), the presentation of heaven as a "marriage feast" (Matthew 22:2), and the most obvious

of all, the Last Supper (see Matthew 26:20–29), point to the
need for considering food, meals, and feeding people in a human
way *before* dogmatizing it in a sacramental way. It seems that
Jesus wanted his listeners to appreciate food for what it means
to humanity—health, healing, community, family, friendship, a
sense of commemoration and celebration, and a furthering and
elevation of culture. Without an anthropological, sociological,
psychological, and biological appreciation for food, a theologian could limit the impact of the theological dimension of food.

Theologians who focus on the Eucharist only as spiritual food
could separate the recipient into compartments of body, mind,
or spirit, rather than see that person as an integrated whole.
Certainly the Eucharist, given in a bite-sized piece of bread, does
not have as much biological effect as a big loaf or a sandwich.
But it humanly connects people to the Body of Christ through
the communal celebration. While the Eucharist is certainly a
very personal thing, it is at the same time very communal. It
connects the recipient not only to the community present at the
liturgy, but to all of salvation history. Limiting the Eucharist to
only the theological reality creates a tendency in the person to be
as disconnected as the Pharisees, scribes, Sadducees, and other
"experts of religious law." They knew the letter of the law, but
didn't know how to practice its spirit when it came to relationships. They used food (in the law) as a weapon that hurt people's
relationships with God and each other, rather than understand
that the law (and food) is something that can heal and strengthen
relationships with God and with each other. Here, my purpose
is simply to remind you that Jesus didn't give us a sacramental

theology of the Eucharist. Instead he gave us a theology of food to prepare us for the Eucharist.

As we understand this teaching about the way God uses food in salvation history, we will see how Jesus's food theology was lifted up, transformed, and changed in substance when the Son of Man was lifted up on the cross, much like the image of the seraph serpent on a pole and the bread elevated by the priest (see Numbers 21:8; John 12:32). Jesus's theological understanding of food was crucified with him. He was crushed like wheat, and his blood was poured out like wine; he was slaughtered in a holocaust and consumed as the innocent Lamb of God.

But that's not the end of the story. He rose from the dead. On the third day, his teachings about food also were elevated to more than just a human reality. As the Body and Blood of Jesus were transformed, so too was his food theology. The power of God transubstantiated Jesus's broken body into the resurrected body. His words about food became the Word that has become food for the soul.

Even after the Resurrection, Jesus's connection to food added another unique chapter in salvation history. As the hungry flock continues the pilgrimage back to the original land flowing with milk and honey, Jesus provides his followers with an opportunity to experience the presence of the ascended Christ each time they "break bread" (see Luke 24:35) and lovingly "feed the sheep" (see John 21:17).

SOMETHING TO CHEW ON
Lamb, fish, and bread were culinary reminders of Jesus for the early Christians. That's what they ate. These foods were

probably also part of Jesus's diet at his home in Nazareth. If Mary prepared fish for a meal, as part of the Jewish community and a Mediterranean race, she more than likely prepared the fish whole!

Nose-to-tail preparation of a fish is an easy way to reclaim rustic cooking techniques, while elevating flavors. Cooking fish with the bones, just like any other protein, imparts greater flavor. Cooking a fish whole with the bones also helps to determine doneness—that is, when the fish is properly cooked. When you roast a fish whole, you can determine if the flesh is fully cooked by tugging on the bones of the fins. If the bone comes out easily and clean, you know the fish is cooked! If you pull on the bones and they don't come out easily, then the flesh hasn't heated enough to release its natural oils and expand.

It's also easier to fillet a fish after it's cooked than while it's still raw. Try it! And when you do, consider how Christ ate a piece of baked fish in the Upper Room after his Resurrection. We become more like Jesus, not just by imitating what he ate, but by eating his very Flesh and Blood in the Eucharist.

PRACTICAL THEOLOGY FOR THE DINNER TABLE

1. How would you describe a theology of food to your family?
2. Have you encountered God's presence at your dinner table, or at a normal meal outside of the Sacred Meal of the Mass?
3. What biblical food passage in the New Testament speaks to you the most?

4. When was the last time you actually fed your neighbor or an acquaintance? Did this meal lead to a closer relationship—a communion of sorts?

5. If you could ask Jesus to satisfy any particular hunger or desire in your life, what would it be? How would you know that he has answered your prayer?

CHAPTER THREE

Mother Church's Battle to Feed the Father's Children

Almighty and Eternal God, behold I come to the sacrament of Your only-begotten Son, our Lord Jesus Christ.... May I thus receive the Bread of Angels, the King of Kings, the Lord of Lords, with such reverence and humility, contrition and devotion, purity and faith, purpose and intention, as shall aid my soul's salvation. Grant, I beg of You, that I may receive not only the Sacrament of the Body and Blood of our Lord, but also its full grace and power. Give me the grace, most merciful God, to receive the Body of your only Son, our Lord Jesus Christ, born of the Virgin Mary, in such a manner that I may deserve to be intimately united with His mystical Body and to be numbered among His members. Most loving Father, grant that I may behold for all eternity face to face Your beloved Son, whom now, on my pilgrimage, I am about to receive under the sacramental veil, who lives and reigns with You, in the unity of the Holy Spirit, God, world without end. Amen.[2] (St. Thomas Aquinas, Prayer before receiving Holy Communion)

The New Testament provides a unique aspect of salvation history called the Paschal Mystery, also known as the "Life, Death, and Resurrection of Jesus Christ." Within this three-part division, we are given two unique ways that Jesus approaches food. First he develops a *theo-socio-anthropological* approach to food at its most basic and fundamental level. However, after the powerful mystery of the Resurrection, Jesus reveals an even deeper revelation of food: a *sacramental* approach to food. After the Resurrection, food becomes something that not only satisfies the body (health) and mind (a sense of confident well-being), it now has a sacramental character that directs both the body and mind to heaven. In the post-Resurrection phase of Jesus's life, food takes on a deeper, more technically theological focus. In the Old Testament, food sustained God's people in their earthly journey. Now, as Christ became the Passover food in the Last Supper, it will be what sustains and eventually transports people to heaven.

As part of its mission, the Church—the magisterial authority that Christ established—is responsible for developing this revelation about food as the ongoing symbol and sacramental sign of salvation history.

As a teaching authority, the early Church's history showed how food helped them to understand, celebrate, and share their faith with others. This food-centric approach was, in a sense, the earliest form of evangelization.

RESURRECTED FOOD

The post-Resurrection accounts of Christ's revelation are uniquely food related. We briefly mentioned some of these in the last chapter. Here, as the magisterium of the Church unfolds and the early Church discovers more about salvation history, we see the intimate ties of faith and food. The three times that Jesus appeared after the Resurrection all involved participation in and sharing of a meal.

The road to Emmaus: The burning and hungry hearts of the people who joined Jesus as companions eventually saw him in the breaking of the bread (see Luke 24:13–35)

The surprise visit by Jesus in the Upper Room: Here, where the Eucharist had been celebrated, Jesus reveals his first messages to the frightened disciples. "Peace, do not be afraid," and, "Do you have anything to eat?" The disciples' fear flees when they provide Jesus with food, and this fulfills what Christ hungered for on the cross—that they would believe in him, which was more important than all of the bloody sacrifices of the Temple (see Luke 24:36–43).

By the shores of the Sea of Galilee: Here Jesus provides another miraculous catch of fish (see John 21:1–23). When the disciples finally recognize Jesus, they discover that Jesus had a meal of bread and fish ready for them. At that most intimate mealtime discussion, Jesus gives Peter his apostolic mandate, saying three times, "Feed my sheep." These three repetitions granted Peter individualized absolutions for the three times that he denied Jesus. For Jesus, providing food and being a companion for the hungry forgives our personal sins, but more important, it reveals that God is actually still fulfilling his mission: to feed his flock through those who love Jesus.

However, after the Resurrection and Ascension, the divine work of feeding people with the bountiful goodness of God continued through his children, born again from Mother Church.

FEEDING A GROWING FLOCK

As the Church grew in quality and quantity, the early founders of the Christian community struggled with learning *how* to feed God's flock. They discovered just how much of a task it was to feed fickle, immature, and spoiled brats (which is what we all are)—the same lessons the Church continues to learn today. But, if they did it well, as Peter would learn, it would eventually lead to one of the most important lessons about the food and faith analogy: Namely, if you really want to feed someone, you must do so with your very life! In other words, giving people food is relatively easy to do. Even atheists contribute food donations to be philanthropic. But believers feed people by their very witness—their very lives. They give more than food for the body; they feed others' faith by their own witness—that is, martyrdom!

This painful lesson about the cost of feeding the flock ultimately taught the Church about the sacrificial nature of food. Feeding people requires sacrifice! Consider the struggles that Moses endured. See how perfectly Jesus sacrificed in order to feed the flock with his very life. And now, in this unique phase of salvation history, the young Church experienced this sacrifice when they become martyrs for the faith. Their lives nourished the souls of others so they could believe. Their deaths became the bitter herbs of truth—the medicine that would eventually transform the bloodthirsty pagan Roman society into fertile ground where the seeds of faith were sown.

THE FOOD FIGHT CONTINUES

The early Church continued God's food fight in two ways. First, they gave witness and testimony by eating with people and continuing to participate in the Sabbath meal, but in a new way. Second, as Christianity became more accepted by civil authorities, they utilized their freedom and resources to further develop a systematic theological study about the deep implications of food and faith. The witness and experience of the early Christians showed the development of a theology of food in concrete and tangible ways, which I will briefly describe here.

Peter and Paul's Shepherding Responsibility (1 Corinthians 5:7; 11:23). Early in the life of the Church, Christians identified themselves by celebrating the Passover feast on a new day. Early Church documents, such as the *Didache*, demonstrate remarkable food and faith connections, evidenced by how the believers shared a liturgy that climaxed with eating the communal meal, and also by mandating that appointed members represent the faith by going out and sharing part of that meal with those who were unable to join the family celebration.

God's Culinary Cleanliness (Acts 11). Peter's strict observance of the Jewish dietary laws was ultimately challenged when he was instructed to slaughter and eat previously forbidden foods. In the Acts of the Apostles, the voice from heaven declares that God's creatures are clean, meant to provide sustenance and strength to the human body. Eating other types of food gave the early Church a wider perspective—a global cuisine, in a sense. It taught them humility, because they were instructed to "eat what is set before you" (Luke 10:8). This prepared the early Church to never judge the food others eat, as this would be a hindrance to their missionary activity. They were to be grateful, humble, open to a variety of experiences, which included eating different foods even from foreigners. Thus, a bridge could be forged to offer conversion through the simple table conversation.

Maturing in Their Food Experiences (Acts 15). After St. Paul's remarkable conversion, a taste of humble pie, with its food and faith implications, took on a more universal dimension. St. Paul became a missionary to the nations, indicating his willingness to not only eat different foods, but also eat with different people—people who at one point of his life were thought to be "unclean," "unworthy," and possible "enemies." His example of eating with others, just as Jesus did with undesirables and public sinners, makes St. Paul a very unique expert in food and faith studies. St. Paul's expertise admonished and convinced St. Peter and the other disciples that, in order to be a true follower of Jesus, they must teach the faith in a new way—a way that invites, not excludes (see Galatians 2:14). St. Paul in effect echoes Jesus's parable of going anywhere and everywhere to invite people to the king's wedding banquet for his son (see Matthew 22:1–14), which eventually became known theologically as the "Great Commission" (see Matthew 28). The whole world is invited to the banquet of the lamb; God doesn't just want to save the chosen people, he seeks to save *all* people. His providence and omnipotent fatherhood universally extends his paternal responsibility to feed every child that enters into the world. He is the universal Father of all. And the word "universal" implies "catholic."

A Universal Invitation

In Catholicism, this universal invitation to a new Way, Truth, and Life requires a process called the Rites of Initiation. The Church's growth obviously required rites of passages before allowing people to partake of the most Sacred Meal (Eucharist), the sign of a true believer. These growing pains came by way of a tension that the early Church had to solve. How could believers extend a universal call to share in the Supper of the Lamb without throwing pearls to the swine? (see Matthew 7:6). This tension is one that Jesus himself considered when he said that the unprepared and underdressed guests that showed up at the banquet would be tossed out in the dark, wailing and screaming (see Matthew 22:10). Jesus also taught that before anyone could leave an offering of food at the Lord's Table, he first needed to reconcile and be in communion with his brother (see Matthew 5:24). And finally, a new twist to the Prodigal Son parable is the process of *metanoia* (i.e., conversion) that the son went through before he considered himself worthy to be under his father's roof and eat with his family again (see Luke 15:11–32).

The responsibility of the early Church, in an effort to universally invite all to the table while protecting the sacred deposit (the Body and Blood of Christ) provided structures and rites of passage so that those who ate the sacred food would know what (really *who*) they were eating. As such, the partakers become believers of an unspoken but universally accepted truth: You are what you eat!

Becoming What We Receive, Celebrate, and Eat

Those who wanted to become Christians would undergo the scrutiny of the teachers during the Rites of Initiation in order to prepare them to receive the sacraments of baptism, confirmation, and Eucharist. The theology of these rites offers a very peculiar culinary perspective.

Baptism requires water. Confirmation requires fire and oil. The Eucharist requires bread and wine. These obvious food implications have a much deeper significance: Christians must *become* what they receive. I'll leave it to systematic theologians to explain how these sacraments adhere to a person, leaving an indelible character in their soul as God's beloved child. For now, though, a culinary perspective can help us understand the conforming and substantially changing qualities (i.e., *transubstantial* elements) of these initiating rites.

Baptism

When a person is baptized—which theologically means that person is dead to sin, he experiences an immersion, or a drowning, in the water of grace. After he rises from the waters, that person is truly living a new life. He no longer reeks from the stench of sin, but instead has been drowned in the renewed waters of Noah's time and will eventually offer himself as a pleasing sacrifice, an aroma of sanctity worthy of God (see Genesis 5—10). In other words, we need to "smell" good enough to eat.

In baptism, sin has also been drowned by the waters of the Red Sea; just like the Israelites, believers escape the slavery of sin and experience a new freedom, unharmed (see Exodus 14).

Finally, baptism allows believers to quench their thirst and drink the pure water made holy by Jesus's immersion into the River Jordan (see Matthew 3). Now they drink freely from the waters of a new Meriba, where Moses called for miraculous water from the rock (see Numbers 20:13; John 4:14).

Confirmation

From a biological point of view, a person drowns when they drink so much water that it gets in their lungs. Our lungs are meant to take in air, not water, which is why confirmation immediately follows baptism. The confirmation rite uses olive oil, infused with perfumed Chrism. In order for this to be sealed by the Spirit, the bishop's authority mimics the prophetic gesture of *breathing* into the oil. As God breathed life into Adam and Jesus breathed on his disciples, the bishop breathes on the oil, which then gives new life to the lungs of the recently "drowned" or "immersed" person (that is, the baptized person). Ritually, the *confirmandi* is doused with this perfumed oil. It corresponds to the anointing that Jesus's lifeless body received before it was placed in the tomb. From the culinary perspective, these elements evoke an image of the beginning of baking bread.

Consider how bread is made—the combination of oil, water, and wheat. This bread also can be understood as the Christian himself. The Christian's body experiences a kind of "crushing" as it is immersed in the baptismal waters, as wheat is crushed and separated from the chaff. St. Ignatius the Martyr gave a striking image of this when he declared how he desired to be the "wheat, crushed by the teeth of the lions"—an indication of the type of death he would face for his beliefs. He was killed and eaten by lions in the Roman circus as a way to appease the Roman emperor's pagan gods. Grapes provide another image of this. As they are crushed, grapes release their juice and eventually, through the mysterious process of fermentation, become wine. This crushing of the grapes provides a framework for understanding the pain and anguish of contrition, which etymologically implies a *con-terre* (with the earth): the crushing of the grapes against the earth.

The Eucharist

The Christian eventually prepares himself to receive the Bread and Wine of the Eucharist and eventually becomes that food. The humble and contrite Christian becomes, if you will, the crushed wheat, combined with oil, infused with the sweet smelling aroma of Chrism, the water of baptism, and the leavening of the breath of Christ from the confirmation oils. These are basic ingredients of bread making! By way of analogy, these elements also form the Christian life. The triple immersion in the waters of baptism, which early Christians considered the "womb and the tomb" evokes the image of the Christian entering his own tomb, which many considered an allegory of an oven or furnace where the elements and combination of ingredients are transformed. Then, after a period of time in this archetypal furnace-tomb, where normally the body becomes ashes, this sacred burial causes the Christian not to be destroyed but rather purified and perfected. The Christian becomes a symbol of one who has shared in the one Bread and one Cup. The Christian becomes one with the

Living Bread of Heaven. Spiritually, he *becomes* what he has eaten from the Lord's Table.

The early Christians, especially the martyrs, realized that if they were to participate in the meal, they had to do so with their entire being. They knew the meal was not simply to satisfy the body but was an indicator for their soul, and vice versa. After the period of teaching, (now known as the Rite of Christian Initiation for Adults, or RCIA), candidates for the new Christian way of life understood that they would have to imitate Christ.

Jesus Christ's body was crushed like wheat, he experienced death by asphyxiation (i.e., water in the lungs), and he gave his last breath as the leaven of his prayer, anointed with the sacred Chrism. His blood was poured out like wine. He was placed gently in the tomb in the same way a baker carefully places dough in the oven. And in three days—at the appointed time—he would exit as a new creation, revealing himself to be the Resurrection and the Life. The food he gave during his human life will now be elevated to a new food in his eternal life.

Rules, Rubrics, and Recipes for Valid Faith

Over the years the Church has sought ways to better define the faith, especially the sacraments (and in particular the Eucharist), with more precisely articulated terms. One way they have given a clearer definition of the Eucharist has been through divine worship—that is, liturgical acts and the formulation of rituals. The participation in these sacred signs laid the foundation for the ecclesial and theological structures to define exactly what "food" the community received at each liturgy. Is it just bread and wine for all? Or is it something more substantial for the many?

The Church continued to see itself as a family, evidenced by the partaking of the Sacred Feast. However, the Church had to determine who should receive this special meal, and how they should receive it. This created a level of anxiety for many that still persists. Even today, people assume that anyone, without any preparation, should be able to eat the Sacred Species. This is a breakdown in understanding the Church's history. Prior to modernity, the Church possessed the full responsibility, as custodians of the faith, to define what people should believe about the Eucharist, who should receive it, and how to participate in this sacred feast.

During the Middle Ages and the period of Scholastics, the Church showed a natural tendency to reinforce the early Christian's desire to first educate the masses before allowing them into the king's banquet hall. They were required to "dress properly" to share in the feast—that is, to be prepared internally and externally. The rules and regulations defined the dignity of the Eucharist. Without this scrupulous approach, the great mystery of the Eucharist easily could be abused. It could be disdained, disrespected, and treated with sacrilege or even irrelevance. The Church's theologians, priests, religious, bishops, and popes provided liturgical reforms regarding the Eucharist to help everyone better understand this unique food, which not *everyone, but many* are permitted to share.[3]

Lex orandi, lex credendi (the law of prayer establishes the law of belief) became a liturgical axiom regarding the Eucharist as food. *What we pray* establishes and informs us about *what we believe*. The Church developed the necessary technical language to describe the lofty understanding of this particular food. Its preparation implicitly required clear guidelines, rubrics, and canonical legalities to protect against abuses regarding the celebration and reception of the Eucharist. The precision of the Eucharistic prayers established a belief about who could legitimately prepare the Eucharist. The prayers based on Scripture, tradition, and magisterial teaching required that only bread from wheat and wine from grapes be used for the liturgy of the Eucharist. Anything else would render the celebration invalid. The proper "matter"—unleavened bread and wine with a significant alcohol level—indicated that the different ecclesial communities would be rooted together in a tradition, one established by liturgical laws and norms. To this day, this provides a sense of unity among the various ecclesial communities in different countries and cultures. A priest who consciously or intentionally uses anything else—for example, using pretzels and soda in an attempt to be more relevant to contemporary society—could be subject to censure and even merit removal from the priesthood.

The particular rubrics for the confection (preparation) of the Eucharist, from a food perspective, show a hierarchical organization as well as a need for adherence to the recipe. Just as well-run kitchens need divisions between executive chefs, sous chefs, chefs du cuisine, and prep and line cooks, so too does the Church. Therefore, any man legitimately ordained to the priesthood has the same responsibility in feeding the flock. Being obedient to the recipe—that is, using the proper form of bread and wine, the recitation of official prayers, and employing the proper gestures assures the congregation that what they are receiving is what they expect: the Eucharist and not some cheap imitation of it.

A strict adherence to the recipe also helps the priest realize that, despite his own unworthiness, if he has the intention to fulfill his obligation and bring about the Eucharist at Mass and if he follows the recipe, he will in fact do just that. Another liturgical axiom, *ex opere operato,* means "the work is worked" and explains how a priest, despite his unworthiness, can still give the flock the Bread of Life. While he may be plagued with sin and even doubt, his honest intention, the mandate from his ordination, and his obedience to the prescribed rubrics will indeed bring the Holy Spirit upon the elements who *changes them* (transubstantiation) into the Body and Blood of Christ— the Food craved by all on this pilgrimage to heaven.

A MIRACULOUSLY MEANINGFUL MEAL

The best example of this undeniable aspect of the faith is the famous Eucharistic miracle of Bolsena-Orvieto in 1263. In this miraculous account, a priest from Bohemia went to Rome on pilgrimage because he doubted the Eucharist and wanted to strengthen his faith. At one point during his pilgrimage, he celebrated Mass in the small town of Bolsena, near Orvieto, Italy. Although he was filled with doubt, confusion, and a weakened faith, he was obedient to the "recipe," celebrating the Mass and following the rubrics and words. When he was elevating the bread, it miraculously transformed into actual flesh, and the wine in the chalice turned into blood. Subsequent investigations of the Church and even those conducted by modern secular scientists confirm that something unexplainable occurred with this "bread/flesh" and "wine/blood." For the Church, this extraordinary event became known as one of the many approved Eucharistic miracles—showing us that the bread and wine are really what Jesus Christ claimed it to be: his Body and Blood.

MERCIFUL MEALS

Throughout the history of the Eucharist, the magisterium has explained God's preeminent desire to feed his children. But this "feeding," as understood through the pastoral guidance of the Church, requires more than a desire to eat and receive this sacred food. The Church requires a penitent to make a public amendment for his or her sins before participating in the Sacred Meal. Scripture backs this up by stating the need for a man to reconcile with his brother before leaving his offerings at the altar (see Matthew 5:23). This, along with the story of the Prodigal Son's confession (see Luke 15:19), applies to each member of the ecclesial community. It hearkens back to the original under-standing of forgiveness before feasting, as evidenced by the powerful story of Joseph extending mercy to the brothers who abandoned him for dead. In his love and mercy, he shared his food with the siblings who realized the famine in their land was a type of divine punishment—a result of their sinful act of selling their brother to slavery. The dramatic account of reconciliation, motivated by a human hunger, shows that a humble confession before God can lead to an absolution, a holy reunion. And in the case of Joseph, his brothers, and his beloved father, it became a true holy communion of persons—all because of a desire to eat (see Genesis 41:55 ff).

The Church established the practice of going to confession, intentionally seeking to make sure that the state of one's soul is as worthy as possible to receive the divine presence of God in that sacred Food. In fact, St. Paul suggests that if we eat this sacred meal without being prepared spiritually, it could have a more "dangerous" effect (see 1 Corinthians 11:27). Doing so would be considered "abusive," in that we would be eating something we weren't supposed to—similar to digesting a powerful medication when we don't need it or deserve it. On a pastoral note, while people may suggest that sinners are sick and need a doctor, the example of Jesus is quite clear: Before we eat this sacred bread, we first need to be reconciled—healed from our sins—through the sacrament of penance.

However, if a person is unable to receive Holy Communion because of sickness, either physical or spiritual, the Church has organized a pastoral response. In the case of physical illness, a prescribed member of the parish brings Communion to the one who is sick as a sign of fellowship and healing. This is a very powerful statement that God is not limited to the four walls of the church. The viaticum, as explained before, is a real demonstration of how God's Food is the ultimate weapon in the divine fight to save souls.

Seeing Is the Believing that Leads to Hungering

For a person who is spiritually unworthy to receive Holy Communion, however, the Church offers yet another opportunity to celebrate the Eucharist through a ritual called Eucharistic Adoration. Its history and tradition, well documented over the early centuries of the Church, became more formalized in the eleventh century. In some cases during the Middle Ages, priests would elevate the consecrated host and wine-filled chalice for an extended period of time for the spiritual benefit of those unable to receive Communion. At one point in the Church's history, people received Communion only once per year; this was known as the "Easter duty." The extended elevation of the Sacred Species provided participants with an opportunity to lift their hearts and minds and receive a spiritual communion. It gave them an opportunity to hunger for Communion, even if they could not receive it physically.

Throughout history, people have always made it a point to visit Catholic churches for personal prayer, to light a candle, and to make a visit to the Blessed Sacrament—the divine presence of the Lord that remains in decorated tabernacles in the church. A sanctuary lamp, a practice that continues today, indicates the presence of these leftover Communion fragments from the divine liturgy. As people worshiped the contents of the ark of the covenant, so too have the faithful over the centuries sought to be in the presence of the Sacred Hosts.

This spiritual visit has grown into the formal ritual, the Exposition of the Blessed Sacrament. From the Latin word *monstrare*, meaning "to show," this ritual created an opportunity for people to worship the presence of the divine Lord in the Eucharist. The consecrated host is placed in a monstrance, a highly decorated vessel used to expose the host to those who, like the Magi, want to adore the presence of Christ. (I refer to the Magi's visit as the first Eucharistic Adoration in history.) Just as Mary, the most beautiful of vessels, holds the Christ child for the adoration of her cousin Elizabeth at the Visitation and then for the Magi and the shepherds, the modern monstrance also provides the rich and poor alike an opportunity to silently be the Lord's companionship. This silent prayer has developed into the pious practice of the Holy Hour, responding to the Lord's invitation at the Garden of Gethsemane, "So, could you not watch with me one hour?" (Matthew 26:40).

From a culinary point of view, Exposition and Adoration of the Blessed Sacrament creates a hunger for us to receive the Eucharist. As people automatically get a bit hungry from watching a cooking show or commercials advertising succulent food, Adoration creates a greater hunger for us to participate more deeply and profoundly in the sacred liturgy where we do more than look at the food. Instead, we receive it!

A Universal Meal or a Divided Dinner?

The regular participation in the Sacred Meal on the Lord's Day has given the Church a sense of unity throughout salvation history. Holy Communion—that is, unity in God's holy family—is Mother Church's effort to prolong and extend God's desire to feed children with the food of salvation and to bring his flock to the eternal banquet.

However, while God's efforts bring the family together, the ancient enemy does everything to destroy that communion, by separating people through sin, distracting them from making time for the liturgy, or through pride and ignorance by suggesting that the Communion is nothing more than a wafer!

Division, the exact opposite of the Communion, is another important turn in salvation history. The food fight continues! The separation from the Lord's Table has taken the form of schisms, reformations, atheistic modernism, internal ecclesial corruption, and secular relativism. The Sacred Meal, over the centuries, has experienced (and will continue to experience) people coming and going. People approach the Sacred Meal, some worthily and some antagonistically. Just like someone leaves the dinner table in a fit of anger, the Church's family meal has also felt that same painful exit of some of its members.

While the separation between members of the flock is a constant sign of the devil's power to entice people as he did Adam and Eve, the Church continues to provide a powerful force to perpetuate God's ability to feed his flock. By Christ's mandate and the Church's liturgies, the food fight will continue to be waged by those on the frontlines: members of the sacred priesthood, those entrusted to shepherd the flock and lead the sheep to verdant pastures. It is because of these priests of Jesus Christ that the heavenly food fight continues.

SOMETHING TO CHEW ON

Why not make bread from another culture or religion for an appropriate interreligious experience? Notice I said "appropriate," because it wouldn't be appropriate to just jump into some other religion's worship or liturgy and assume we can fully take part in it. Also notice I didn't suggest that you "bake bread," because *baking* isn't the only way to *make* bread. But as one way to experience the Jewish culture, consider making unleavened, or even *challah,* bread. Or, you might consider serving an Indian naan bread to start a conversation about monotheism of the Jewish, Christians, and Muslims in comparison to the piety of polytheism of our Hindu brothers and sisters. Making Thai-style bread (called *roti)* can provide an opportunity to discuss whether Buddha would describe Buddhism as a *religion* (in a strict definition) or a *philosophy*—a way of life. Interestingly enough, Muslims also call their pan-fried bread *roti.*

It's also an edifying experience to make different breads within the Christian tradition—religious-inspired Bavarian *pretzels,* feast day Polish *babka b*read, or Byzantine *antidoron* used in the liturgy as "blessed" but not "consecrated" bread. This will certainly inspire honest talk about the different forms of communion within the Christian tradition. In this exercise, participants discover the need for precision in bread making— i.e., following the recipe *exactly!* At the same time, eating bread, while a generic act, requires "precision" in understanding (and respecting) the Catholic Church's teaching regarding the sacred Eucharistic host as form of "super-substantial" (i.e., non-ordinary) bread. Bread represents universality. Every culture has it— even if they use different types of flour, cooking techniques, or spiritual motivation. But in the case of Roman Catholicism, the fact that Jesus becomes the Bread of Life shows a unique experience of God. The children of the world become one family in faith, sharing one Bread and one Cup, truly becoming one— with each other and with him. The theology of food as well as the theology of the sacrament of the Eucharist is best understood when we recognize the complexity of simple foods, such as the crumbs that fell from the master's table (see Matthew 15:27).

PRACTICAL THEOLOGY FOR THE DINNER TABLE

1. What have you done to share your Catholic faith in the Eucharist with others?
2. What Eucharistic experiences have you had that confirmed your faith in it?
3. How do the prayers and gestures at Mass affirm the sacred nature of the Eucharist?
4. Do you think it's fair or unfair, just or unjust, theologically correct or incorrect, that non-Catholics cannot receive Communion? How do you explain this to others?
5. What do you think Jesus would say about your parish's particular celebration of the Eucharist? Would he be pleased? Why or why not?

CHAPTER FOUR

The Front Lines
of the Food Fight
• • •
The Sacred Priesthood

When they had finished breakfast, Jesus said to Simon Peter, "Simon, son of John, do you love me more than these?" He said to him, "Yes, Lord, you know that I love you." He said to him, "Feed my lambs." A second time he said to him, "Simon, son of John, do you love me?" He said to him, "Yes, Lord, you know that I love you." He said to him, "Tend my sheep." He said to him the third time, "Simon, son of John, do you love me?" Peter was grieved because he said to him the third time, "Do you love me?" And he said to him, "Lord, you know everything; you know that I love you." Jesus said to him, "Feed my sheep. Truly, truly, I say to you, when you were young, you girded yourself and walked where you would; but when you are old, you will stretch out your hands, and another will gird you and carry you where you do not wish to go." (This he said to show by what death he was to glorify God.) And after this he said to him, "Follow me." (John 21:15–19)

As in any battle, there is a front line where certain members of the rank take a very active and dangerous role. In this battle for souls, the sacred priesthood of Jesus Christ can truly be understood as those members who have the responsibility to feed the flock with the divine Food.

The local parish priest, while a very common figure for the faithful, actually has a more intense role than people imagine. The priest fights on the front lines. He stands at a unique place during salvation's history. Continuing the custom of the Jewish Scripture regarding the priesthood, the bloodline of priests was responsible for offering the sacrifice to placate God, to fulfill the command to make the proper offering, and to sanctify man as a way to protect him from evil, harm, and the imbalanced forces of the world, such as plagues, drought, or other disasters that create hunger on a mass scale.

In the New Testament however, with the destruction of the Temple, the priesthood takes on a different character—but the important elements of establishing a relationship between God and his people continue. In a new way, however, the priesthood was evidenced in the person of the high priest Melchizedek, a figure whose origin and purpose remains as mysterious as the priesthood of Jesus Christ (see Genesis 14:18 and Hebrews 7:1–10). As Jesus was not part of the priestly lineage (although he had ties to King David through his foster father Joseph), Jesus is understood as the high priest in the New Testament because of his ability to sanctify—that is, dedicating the common things to God and making the ordinary holy. This would include curing the sick, teaching profound truths with a unique authority unlike the scribes and Pharisees, and ultimately feeding the people with more than bread from heaven. He will feed them with the Bread of Life: his own flesh and blood. Jesus's priestly character is made quite evident by the fact that he performs the ultimate priestly sacrifice. Yet he goes one step further in this salvific process: He becomes the sacrificial victim.

SALVATION: A PRIESTLY ACT

The self-giving and self-donation of Christ as the Bread of Life and the Cup of Salvation points to a unique character about the role of food in salvation history: It is a priestly act. The food that Jesus gave to people, either for the body or the soul, established an intimacy—a tight connection with them. Remember how the apostles began to believe in Jesus when he changed water into wine? How the people wanted to proclaim him king at the miracle of the multiplication of the loaves and fishes? Food, in the hands of Jesus the high priest becomes that instrument of grace through which miracles are made and profound teaching is offered. This food not only satisfies the requirement to serve God, it also satisfies the hunger of God's people.

Does this intimacy between God and his people end at the point of the Ascension, when Jesus mounts his throne in heaven? No! In fact, salvation history takes a whole different turn, a sort of new beginning. At the very least, it begins a new mission of feeding the flock—but in a new way, through the newly appointed shepherds.

Instead of the line-by-line, person-to-person evangelization Jesus employed, he first appointed twelve men, then seventy-two to go throughout the entire world and share the Good News. As he predicted, the fishermen would now be responsible for catching humanity in the nets of God's enfolding love. They would be fishing for souls (see Matthew 4:19).

And how will this catching for the Lord be done? You guessed it, through the priesthood. The connection between the priesthood and salvation history is evidenced by the mandate to evangelize the world, inviting many to the Lord's Table and transmitting the faith through the Paschal Mystery commemorated at each Eucharistic liturgy with the words, "When we eat this Bread and drink this Cup, we proclaim your Death, O Lord, until you come again."

This commemoration of the Last Supper through the hands of the priest is efficacious in many ways, but I'll highlight just two. First, it enables people to worship correctly and be confidently incorporated into God's family. Remember, God has one desire: to feed his people the food to make them into saints in heaven. This is, in a sense, a way to glorify God—that is, to eat what God sets before us as the gift of the finest wheat. The sacred liturgy celebrated by the priest provides all nations with the opportunity to come together and be fed by God through the sacred priesthood of Jesus Christ. When we eat the bread and drink the cup at Mass, we are sacramentally transported to the moment of the Last Supper. The commemoration at Mass is really a participation in the first (and only) Last Supper. Those who participate in the Eucharist are as present to Jesus as he is to them. The power of the priesthood, instituted by Jesus Christ, provides even the most common believer with an opportunity to experience extraordinary holiness! This is a major consideration for the personal part each person plays in salvation history. The

Eucharistic celebration at each parish Mass continues what Jesus initiated, the one saving act of God. At some place in the world, *even at this very moment*, a priest is celebrating the sacred rites and remembering Jesus as he instructed us—through the Bread and Wine. Therefore, one very particular way this Last Supper is efficacious is that we become intimately a part of the Last Supper as Christ intended—a foretaste of the heavenly banquet.

By not going to church, we step away from the opportunity to be saved. It is safe to say that freely choosing to deny ourselves of the Eucharist is a way *not* to get into heaven. "Unless you eat the flesh of the Son of man and drink his blood, you have no life in you" (John 6:53). That's what a priest's job is: to feed you the food that will get you to heaven! That job is much more difficult—and dangerous—than people assume. Try feeding a spoiled child good food. Try feeding an antidote to a sick animal!

Another efficacious quality of the Eucharist is the sign of Communion that brings every nation into one Holy Communion, a true unity—God's desire from the first moment of salvation history: to bring all into his communal love! No other institution in world history can boast of the unity established by the Roman Catholic Church's approach to the celebration of the Last Supper. From a practical point of view, a priest within the Roman Rite can celebrate and commemorate the Lord's Last Supper wherever he is in the world. The people generally know the responses. The Mass, though it externally may have some differences, is substantially the same. When the priest, in whatever language, offers the host and chalice to a communicant, the recipient knows the answer in every language: *Amen!* It's a statement that agrees with the priest: It truly is the Body and Blood of Christ! This unity provides the Church with a significant advantage over the enemy in the fight for souls in salvation history. The Church, like a mother hen, seeks to gather her flock under the wings of her protective mantle (see Luke 13:34). It's the priest's vocation to go out, announce the invitation, and shepherd others through the rites of initiation to the Lord's celebration. It's the priest's responsibility to bring about unity through communion.

On the other hand, the Evil One seeks only to destroy the sources of communion. He convinces people that the Eucharist is just "a piece of bread or sip of wine" and not the substantial presence of the divine Lord, or he distracts them and occupies their attention with an overly busy schedule, causing them to rush through this sacred meal with the same under-appreciation of eating fast food or skipping the meal altogether. When we don't take time to nurture our relationship with the Eucharist, we begin to treat the liturgy as fast food. The priest is seen as doing nothing more than dispensing food to lazy, dependent people who care very little *how* they eat and *what* they eat, or *who* may be serving them a delicious-looking forbidden food. The surveys show that we don't see the Eucharist as anything special; we don't see the priesthood as God's frontline fighters!

SPIRITUAL FATHERS FEEDING OUR FATHER'S FAMILY

This chapter, obviously, is dedicated to the priesthood—the shepherds who collaborate with the Holy Spirit in feeding the flock. However, this isn't a "how to be a better priest" chapter, as I'm certainly not worthy to give fail-safe advice. Instead, I can offer a perspective that has become increasingly more relevant for me as I develop this theology of food in consideration of my personal priesthood. At the same time, this chapter is also meant to be of special help to the flock—the parishioners—to learn how to be a better member of the fold. By learning more about the priesthood's intimate relationship with food, the people in the pews can become better members of the Church, more engaged members of the flock, and more receptive to the call of the shepherd—the man we call father, monsignor, bishop, or pope.

These clergy members are only men, but by their ordination they have a special connection to food that, if understood well, is very helpful in feeding a finicky flock. It's not easy to do. Just ask Moses as he tried to herd the Israelites in the desert. Consider Jesus's Good Shepherding skills which proved so successful until the wolf came and scattered the sheep, simply because there was no one to shepherd and protect them (Matthew 26:31). Priests are put on the front lines to wield the staff and to call the flock to verdant pastures and still waters. The connections between the priesthood, food, and faith need more theological development with pastoral insight.

LIKE FATHER, LIKE FLOCK

Let's consider the priest's personal approach to food. Oftentimes you can see a connection in how a man's earthly view of food connects to the heavenly food. If a priest is sloppy in his diet, reliant on fast food, unhealthy in his personal eating habits, and careless about the formalities of dining versus eating, we sometimes see that same sloppiness, lack of care, and unhealthy approach in the way that priest celebrates Mass. This obviously is not a perfect correlation, but it's definitely worth considering as anecdotal evidence that a priest who has a healthy understanding of meals will treat the Eucharist with the reverence of a sacred feast.

Catholic Culinary Culture

The symbol of loftiness and grandeur evidenced in the Eucharistic celebration indicates a meal par excellence! It's the type of meal that requires getting cleaned up, dressed up, and mentally and spiritually prepared for. The analogy, though imperfect, is sufficient enough. How would the priest prepare to share a meal at the home of someone famous—the leader of a nation, for example, or the pope? The care taken to prepare for such an earthly meal ought to be transferred to the care a priest takes to celebrate the Eucharistic meal. All too often, though, even a priest can fall into a rut and succumb to schedule demands. He eats on the run, eats alone, and eats a poor and fatty diet. Evidenced by the generally poor health of many priests, we can see that the sloppiness of a priest's personal approach to common food has some correlation as to how he celebrates the Sacred Feast.

Unfortunately, the fast-food mentality has crept into the liturgical mind-set of many Catholics, resulting in a flock that is content with a fast-food approach to the Sacred Meal. Mass, for them, is an experience of "in and out in one hour or less." They become finicky and testy, as children forced to behave at a formal dinner. They would rather eat junk food than patiently dine on the elegance required for the heavenly foretaste.

The priest must then approach the Sacred Meal with a sense of balance: helping people see the human theology of food and the sacramental theology of the Eucharist at the same time. By his own personal understanding, he must show the people the care with which he approaches the Sacred Feast, which in turn becomes a loud reminder for how the parishioners ought to approach the altar. If the priest is rushed, sloppy, seemingly distracted and uncaring, dressed shabbily (not seeming to consider personal comportment necessary for something sacred), then it's no surprise that the flock approaches Mass the same way. If the priest doesn't care, why should the people?

TABLE FOR ONE?

Another consideration: with whom does the priest eat? Does he initiate opportunities for priestly gatherings? Does he avoid invitations for fraternal dinners? How often does he eat alone and does he monitor his food and drink intake responsibly? The busy priestly schedule oftentimes leads too many priests to eat alone, oftentimes willfully choosing *not* to share a meal with their brother priests. This is dysfunctional, and it affects a priest's pastoral skill. He becomes a loner! If he can't build fraternity and community with other priests as friends and spiritual brothers, how will he develop community and fellowship with the strangers he refers to as "parishioners"? The idea of priests being able to offer hospitality and be good dinner companions is rooted in those very words. By offering hospitality, the priest offers a type of "hospital"—a place in the church home to bring healing to hungry souls. If he can learn to be a good dinner companion, the priest then becomes one with those whom he breaks bread, and like the disciples on the road to Emmaus, he experiences the presence of Christ in the breaking of the bread.

A Priestly Challenge: A Balanced Diet

Priests should seek to develop a deeper appreciation for earthly food as a *symbol or a sacramental* (i.e., not a sacramental sign or sacrament) that serves as a means to an end. They can be encouraged, no matter how simple their background, to learn how to formally approach a meal. For instance, consider St. John Vianney, a simple priest with a low-income upbringing. When it came to the Eucharist, he used only the most ornate and precious metal for a chalice, the finest fabric and designs for altar cloths and vestments. He treated the rites of the liturgy with such care and compassion that his flock began to appreciate and hunger for the Eucharistic food due to his example. He knew how to feast with the goodness of the Lord, even though he fasted regularly throughout his entire life.

At the same time, a priest's *formality* should never obscure the *familiarity* of this meal. The liturgy should never be something so formal that simple and humble saints wouldn't recognize it because of the elaborate trappings. Each priest must examine his conscience and see if there is balance in his appreciation for the sacred vessels and what those vessels contain. Priests sometimes can focus too much on the chalice, paten, and other accessories of the liturgy and forget that these beautiful, ornate vessels are meant for the One who is held in them. It's not for the priest himself. The balance is a difficult one. A priest must show, by his own approach to food, the dignity and the simplicity of the Mass, the formality and the familiarity of the ritual, and demonstrate the lofty supernatural food of the Eucharist while recognizing it as simple unleavened bread and table wine.

During my teaching days at a seminary, I had the difficult task of teaching a class called "Priest as a Public Person," which instructed seminarians in all the basics of human and personal formation. It included reminders about how to dress, proper hygiene, personal health and relationships, and yes, how to eat and dine in appropriate settings. Some of the seminarians resisted this, considering it an act of pomposity and contrary to the simplicity of the priesthood. However, it's important that priests know how to eat with the poor and rich alike (see Philippians 4:12)—and more important, how to approach each morsel with gratitude. St. Paul teaches us to see earthly food as a means of more clearly communicating what we believe about the Eucharist as divine food (i.e., a theology of food).

A priestly theology of food suggests that a priest not only knows how to eat but also respects and appreciates the food of different groups of people. He must be able to celebrate foods eaten by poor people, rich people, and foreign people. He won't turn up his nose to poor people's food (i.e., fast food or simple home cooking) because he's too cultured in the fine foods of his age. He will also not turn away opportunities to celebrate fine gourmet or special foods in his attempt to live a simple and humble life. He will learn to eat what is set before him, even if it is a completely different experience than his own, pulling him out of his comfort zone. In this practical understanding of the theology of food, he will have the culture, class, and couth to see how food, well-celebrated and eaten with gratitude and a sense of community, becomes that first step in being able to create a hunger for the supernatural food of God's Table. If he can eat anything with humility, gratitude, and dignity, he can win over the hearts and souls of his dinner companions. They will see him as *one of them* and, as with Jesus's example, they will be more willing to listen to that priest than to other religious figures who choose not to eat with the common people.

A Priestly Part of the Family

Another dimension of this priesthood, food, and faith connection is a priest spending time with his parishioners around a family dinner table. This enables people to see their priest not only as the sacred instrument through which the Eucharist is confected, but also as a "normal" person like them. Like Christ, the priesthood must balance the sacred nature of the meal with all its human reality—setting the table, doing the dishes, and experiencing the struggles of moms and dads to feed their children. In some cultures, having the priest come to the house for dinner is a great honor. It is there that his parishioners see his dignity close up, as well as his humanity. The hosts recognize a familiarity with the man of the cloth, and he then takes the role as the spiritual father at the dinner table, able to share his priesthood through his own humanity by the common act of eating. The act of eating together puts the priest on an even greater level of intimacy with his people. While it could appear to be lowering his stature among the community, it actually increases it. Similar to the way a political campaign relishes the opportunity to be seen eating with the common folk at picnics or barbecues, the priest shares himself in an intimate way, modeling the way Jesus approached his ministry by inviting himself to eat even in the homes of sinners. The more he ate with the common people, the more his authority grew into something new—unlike the scribes and Pharisees who made a point of separating themselves from the common meals of the people. By simply being present to eat with his parishioners outside the Eucharistic banquet, the priest truly becomes a part of the family.

The struggle for a priest to really get to know his parishioners through the family celebrations (i.e., in the context of the domestic church) is understandable. There just isn't enough time to really get to know all of the members of one's flock. With diminishing numbers of priests available, it is easy to see the priest as distant—someone at the altar but not at one's dinner table. Also, past scandals within the priesthood create a natural defense mechanism for a priest and his parishioners. The fear of suspicion and the law can force an attitude of safety through seclusion. He might not want to get to know his parishioners because his friendliness and familiarity somehow might be misconstrued as inappropriate and create a possible legal threat against someone who is simply trying to be a spiritual father to his parish families.

These barriers for a priest to share personally with those in his parish are no doubt a part of the devil's plan to keep the priest as someone separate from the common experience and destroy the communal relationship between the shepherd's familiar voice and the flock he is called to lead. Priests that keep their distance from the family dinner table affect history, and in some cases, the salvation of souls. Just think about what would have happened for the sinners, prostitutes, and tax collectors if Jesus stayed away from them!

Whether you're a parishioner or a priest, consider your own experience with the priests in your parish. Many Catholics don't really know their priests, and many brother priests hardly know each other. Unless a parishioner takes an active approach and becomes involved in the parish, his or her interaction with the priest is typically for only one hour on Sunday. That hour is often very chaotic, with parents struggling to quiet children and others less than interested in what the priest is saying. One's experience of the priesthood all too often is irrelevant, antagonistic, or understandably boring. This couldn't be farther from the truth and reality of the priest, his personhood, or the sacred rites he celebrates.

The one thing that can help a person gain more of an insight into the life of the parish is to get to know priests. At the same time, the priest ought to take a more personal, fatherly role and less of an administrative role. He ought to make himself available for interacting with parishioners—and not only during parish meetings. To say it plainly: He must share meals with them!

While this can be difficult to achieve, it's easy to see that a well-respected priest with a successful parish can develop the ability to balance the professional demands of running a church and the personal requirements to be part of the family dinner table.

On the other hand, when a priest is distanced from his parishioners and the family dinner table, it makes it even harder for him to do what he is called to do: feed the flock. The flock, without a familiar sense of the shepherd's voice, becomes suspicious of the things the priest wants to provide as food for thought. It becomes as difficult as a parent trying to feed children healthy vegetables. The children resist, and even consider their parents as the enemy. Our broken nature takes the same approach in the parental relationship of the Mother Church and the fatherly quality of the priesthood. By the conniving of the devil, feeding the flock becomes a battle for the priest!

A FATHER'S FIRST TASK: TO FEED SOULS

The flock doesn't want to eat, or digest, what the priest is serving. They see the food he offers as something harmful rather than helpful—like the way children approach bitter medicine. This resistance puts enmity between the shepherd and the flock. All the while, the devil is able to tempt the flock from the fold by creating a more attractive exterior to harmful foods. The flock ends up with a diminished ability to discern right from wrong, and the priest himself is unable to make the truth look attractive and worth savoring. He has food to feed, the best food of all—the Eucharist—but the flock won't eat it.

Unless the priest can re-evangelize and re-engage the family, as Jesus did, by meeting them at their own dinner table, he won't have a chance to really catechize them. It is at the dinner table where Jesus taught his greatest lessons about love, compassion, forgiveness, and selflessness. When the priest, so consumed by all of the administrative tasks of his responsibilities, forgets to be a father to his people, his part in the food fight becomes less relevant. The flock won't see the priest's food as worth eating because they won't know him as shepherd and won't care about him as a person. In these distant relationships, the priest becomes a kind of machine that dispenses churchy things.

FATHERLY ADVICE AND FAMILIAR CONVERSATIONS

A priest can better feed his flock through a more focused approach in homiletics. The word *homily* comes from the Greek understanding of "familiar conversation." This describes what the two men walking on the road to Emmaus were doing. They were engaged in a "homily." They weren't preaching to each other; they were sharing a conversation in a familiar way. Jesus enters into that conversation, captivating the listeners to the point that his divine presence is revealed in the breaking of the bread.

The priest's homily is an important form of food for the flock. If the flock is well fed, it will return and not seek other pastures. If the homily is substantial and communicated well, the people will be able to digest and incarnate the teachings from the pulpit. Unfortunately, many complain about the Catholic approach to sermons, preaching, and homilies. They feel they are not being fed, and therefore leave for congregations with better, more skilled, and even more entertaining messengers.

It's important that the priest, working with the food of faith, learns how to present, deliver, and serve the message of truth in a way that makes the flock craving more. From a culinary point of view, the priest, as someone heavily involved in the "food industry," can learn the effective techniques of chefs and specialty cooks in order to mold his ability to deliver the faith to hungry souls. Below is a list of food and faith analogies that could be helpful for the preacher, homilist, and anyone else who is responsible for delivering the Word of God as food for the soul.

Keep the Message Focused and Bite-sized. Provide just enough for the people to chew and digest. New preachers especially tend to give so much information in one homily that people are overwhelmed. It's like taking a sip of water from a fire hydrant! Consider Jesus's approach to preaching. His sermons were relatively short. He got to the point and allowed people to digest his message without overwhelming them. The fact is that people are not trained to hear the truth in its fullness. Many, like infants, can only handle milk and may not be able to digest the substantial meat of the faith (see 1 Corinthians 3:2). While some may think this is a reduction of the gospel message, it's actually recognizing, respecting, accepting, and working with the abilities (and inabilities) of the receiver. Just as we wouldn't give meat to babies, the homilist must take care to not force-feed the flock. They will not be able handle it, they will regurgitate the message, and they will become resentful for being force-fed.

Provide a Balanced Seasoning of the Message. While it's important to serve the bitter herb of truth, it's sometimes easier to serve the truth with a little coating of sweetness. Again, while some may consider this a reductionist approach to homiletics, consider Jesus's approach to teaching. He was so filled with Good News that people wanted more and left feeling good, even if they were challenged. The homilist needs to balance the sweetness of the Good News with the tartness, or bitterness, of the truth. The presentation of the message becomes as important as the substance of the message itself. If a challenging message can be presented in a way that is nonconfrontational, nonargumentative, and less acerbic, then the listener will be more than ready to hear and accept the message.

Sweetness catches more flies than vinegar. That is also true for the Gospel message, which is finer than purest gold and sweeter than honey from the comb (see Psalm 119:103). At the same time, if the preacher only gives sweet messages, his hearers may develop a sweet tooth that can easily lead to cavities and an unhealthy appetite for junk food. Balance is the key to both a good meal and a good spiritual message.

Serve a Fresh Message. Leftover homilies are those that the priest uses over and over again. The redundancy of his message is based in the fact that he has not challenged himself to see the dynamic quality of God's Word. He rehashes a previous homily that is scripted, impersonal, and lackluster. A processed homily can be just as boring as yesterday's leftovers for the flock. These homilies normally come from a homily service that a priest chooses to use. Instead of relying on his own experience or meditation, he serves up someone else's precooked message. Similar to a chef who uses processed food, the priest loses creativity and discipline. Unfortunately, the person who has to digest the message is the one who suffers.

Consider the Timing and Temperature of the Homily. Timing and temperature is as important to cooking as it is for the homilist. This allows for the right amount of heat without overdoing it or underdoing it. Too often people experience homilies that are just too long, leaving them weary, frustrated, and hot tempered. It's every bit as unpleasant as eating meat that that has been overcooked until it's the texture of shoe leather! Conversely, an underwhelming homily can be equally frustrating. Eating undercooked food is dangerous! It also makes people lose their appetite. While people appreciate shorter homilies that are concise and to the point, an overly short homily can leave members of the flock undernourished and underfed. If the flock's hunger is not satisfied on a regular basis, they will be tempted to graze in other pastures by joining other churches, denominations, or even attractive cults.

Plant the Seed (the Word of God) into the Flock's Hearts and Souls. The priest has the responsibility to grow the faith in order to feed the flock with the faith. In effect, the priest is not only shepherd but farmer as well. Most of us are familiar with parable of the sower (see Matthew 13) who spreads the seed to different areas (or states of souls), such as good soil (a fruitful and open soul), rocky soil (a soul hardened by sin), thicket-filled soil (a soul distracted with the material things of the world), and shallow soil (an immature and self-absorbed soul).

This parable contains another food-related lesson for the priest. He knows that the seed is the Word of God, the food that will grow into the fruits of the Holy Spirit. He is reminded that before he can feed the heart, mind, and soul of the listener, he ought to be aware of the various and often difficult states of life of the people in his congregation. The priest is beset by his own weakness. He has only a limited amount of seed to spread. He should be judicious about how he shares the Word of God with others; he must be careful. Before planting God's Word in their hearts, he has to first prepare the soul by clearing away the distractions.

He needs to be aware of where people are—the state of their souls—and work to provide a deeper emotional connection to the faith before trying to instruct his parishioners theologically. Without an emotional connection, the flock won't feel motivated enough to digest the teachings. The homily, in a sense, creates an environment in the soul before planting the seed. And as a farmer prays that God will provide the other necessary elements, such as good weather, the priest must do the same. If the priest does his part, he must trust that God will do his.

* * *

I hope that this chapter will help my readers become more aware of the challenges priests face. My prayer is that you can be more receptive to your priest's homilies, and perhaps reach out to your priest on a more personal level in order to see him as he is—a man called to collaborate in the divine act of self-donation, which is perhaps the most challenging aspect of the relationship between the priest and faith as food. The priest must *become* the food that he consecrates. He uses the words "in persona Christi"—*this is* my *body."* He doesn't say, "This is *Jesus's* Body"; he says, "This is *my* body," indicating the self-sacrifice of his own person. He becomes what he eats intimately on a daily basis. He is a living billboard for the feast to which God calls all of us. He is a real-life commercial for the best food in town—the Eucharistic meal at the local parish. He becomes the wellspring so the thirsty souls can drink (see John 4:14). He is also the lure on the string of the fisherman to catch the fish into the nets of God's love. If the bait is worth eating, it will bring in a large catch. If the priest is not an attractive sign of God's presence—a presence filled with joy, life, and hope—then we can understand why so many churches are empty on weekends.

Theologically, the priest must become the food that fills the ears, hearts, minds, and souls of the parishioners who are daily in the middle of the food fight in salvation history. His must be an authentic meal, which means that he is not merely preaching from his knowledge of the truth, but from his experience of it.

FROM HIS HANDS TO YOUR LIPS

A newly ordained priest offers a "First Blessing" to the faithful, who often then kiss the priest's hand as an indication that his hand is now no longer his own. This is the hand that provides the food of salvation. The priest stands at the crossroads and the front lines of salvation history's epic food fight. He must be strengthened by the food he hopes to give, and he will be victorious when he receives that food with the generous spirit of a well-prepared soul that will grow the Word of God and bear great fruit in him.

When the priest receives the fragments of consecrated Bread and the diluted drops of precious Blood from the Mass, he prays, "May what passes my lips as food be received in purity of heart. May what I receive in time be my remedy in eternity" (*Roman Missal*). The priest becomes a symbol of the meal that God wants to feed each of us. "Behold, I stand at the door and knock; if anyone hears my voice and opens the door, I will come in to him and eat with him" (Revelation 3:20). As Jesus's representative on earth, the priest must now open his soul to his parishioners and invite them to the banquet of love that he shares with the Lord. And with the Lord, there is more than enough to be shared with those who hunger for that intimate supper found in the soul of the faithful and fruitful priest.

Something to Chew On

Getting to know your priest or minister more personally can be a daunting task. They can be so busy, and sometimes you might have an impression of them (good or bad) that makes them seem a bit untouchable. Think about the reasons it can be difficult to have a personal relationship with your local spiritual leader. Then, consider how you can overcome this barrier.

One way to do this is to create an opportunity to gather with a few good friends and simply invite your priest to join you. No agenda, no problems to discuss, no issues to raise—just an opportunity to have a meal together. By simply inviting your local clergy to your home for a meal, without pressure and at a time that is convenient for everyone, you can create more of a family atmosphere for your church. First, find out what the priest prefers to eat, and then create your dinner menu. Be careful not to monopolize the minister's time by being the only family that regularly invites him. Have an open invitation, but extend an occasional invitation—maybe once or twice during the summer and once during the liturgical celebration seasons of Christmas or Easter.

One more consideration: Don't be offended if he declines your invitation. He might be busy, or he just may not feel comfortable at this stage of his service to the community. Give it some time, and make your invitation as attractive as possible without being intrusive. Perhaps you can offer to be part of a team that organizes a parish supper club that provides an opportunity for the entire parish to host a big potluck dinner for whoever wants to come. Again, the only agenda these dinners should have is simply to share a common meal together, get to know each other, and sample different recipes and cuisine. Perhaps there is also a hidden agenda: to have a little family fun!

PRACTICAL THEOLOGY FOR THE DINNER TABLE

1. What parallels can you make between the *spiritual fatherhood* of the priest and the *practical fatherhood* of a dad?

2. What type of priest—or what characteristics of the clergy—feeds your soul the most?

3. How can you personally encourage a better relationship between the Church and the people of God?

4. How is the homily a way for the priest to feed God's people?
5. How is your priest or minister (or how is your priesthood and ministry) similar or dissimilar to that of Jesus Christ?

CHAPTER FIVE

The Consummation of Love at the Eternal Wedding Banquet

Grant, holy Father, that, desiring to approach your table as a couple joined in Marriage in your presence, they may one day have the joy of taking part in your great banquet in heaven. Through Christ our Lord. (Conclusion of Option B of the Nuptial Blessing)

Married couples play a unique role in salvation history. Adam and Eve's spousal love for each other reflected the permanent commitment and communion of the God who made them—one God, three persons—united in an unbreakable and permanent bond of love. The sacred relationship between man and woman, as helper and helpmate and mutual collaborators, can be understood anew through a food-oriented perspective. From this prefigured role, husbands and wives as parents serve on the front lines of the food fight in the domestic church, just as a priest is placed on the front lines of the universal Church.

After the Fall, Adam and Eve were punished by having to till the earth and suffer the pains of pregnancy. Prior to the Fall, everything was provided for this young couple. Their disobedience subjected them to the natural forces that would affect their relationship with each other forever. They would have to work with and work through the agricultural seasons, as well as the seasons of biological fertility. They would know the challenge of bringing life into the world. And they would have the great responsibility to ensure that their children were cared for, protected from the elements—and most important, fed.

Adam and Eve could not have done this alone. Their sinful condition, which limited their strength and capabilities, required a grace-filled helper, a spouse. In fact, in the beginning, God explained his reason for making such a relationship a necessary part of man's journey back to God: "It is not good that the man should be alone" (Genesis 2:18). Man was not created for a solitary life but a communal one. That's true for a celibate priest, but it's especially true for a single man or woman. God wants man to have a companion—someone with whom to share the burden of bringing bread into the world and share its bounty.

A New Phase in God's Plan

Throughout salvation history, the marriage covenant reveals a uniquely new phase in God's plan to defeat the devil and save souls. While the devil seeks to destroy communion among God's people, God constantly creates opportunities for humanity to come together and intimately collaborate with one another to help nourish and nurture one another.

The covenant between great leaders in the Scripture demonstrates an archetype of marriage that brings about either the flourishing or the diminishing of society. As good marriages have helped bring about a positive turn in salvation history, poor marriage decisions or bad relationships have led to destructive tendencies for God's people, and the path back to God's Promised Land is impeded, obstructed, and unclear.

Some examples are: Abraham and Sarah, Noah and his wife, the prescriptions about who to marry found in Leviticus, David's unfortunate obsession with his future wife Bathsheba, the deceitful acts of Onan and his infidelity with his brother's wife— and of course the ultimate blessing of Joseph and Mary's relationship, which shows how the quality of that marriage allowed God's grace to be manifested. Good marriages lead to good experiences; unfaithful relationships bring about punishment, difficult lessons, and challenging ramifications for God's people.

One consistent relationship requirement that God demands from those involved in a covenant of love is *fruitfulness*—"Be fruitful and multiply" (Genesis 1:28). Fruitfulness correlates to God's procreative character. The ability to bring life into the world speaks of God's potency. Children, the fruit of parental love, describe how God desires to be the Father of all. But fruitfulness requires the cooperation of man and woman in an intimate act of sexuality, an act that highlights well the food-and-faith connection when framed within the analogous language of sexual appetite and the hunger for intimacy.

Consider how the same language used to describe one's desire for food is often used to describe the sexual appetite. This language of "appetite," "hunger," and "desire" colors the theological lens when looking at salvation history, because salvation history could be summed up in God's desire to people this earth and—more important—eventually bring those people into the kingdom of heaven. It is undeniable how much God celebrates life. He is a loving Father that takes great delight in his people, desiring to feed them and bring them to himself. This procreative desire of God requires the cooperation of God's children. When God's children comply and cooperate with God, fruitfulness is the result. When God's children do not follow his plan for salvation, the fruit is now spurned.

A Commonsense Approach for the Consummation of a Couple

God created food before he created people. Food would be necessary for people to survive, but people would have to hunger for this food, or it would simply go to waste. As it turned out, Adam and Eve hungered for something not according to God's plan. As part of the punishment for their disobedience, the couple would have to try to be more like God, bringing life into the world and also caring for it. Bringing life into the world requires cooperating with God (he is still in charge, even if Adam and Eve wanted to be). They would have to conform their lives to the nature of the seasons (including the biological season of the woman) making sure to bear fruit by sowing the seed rather than having it spill on infertile ground—an act punishable by death (see Genesis 38:9).

In this context I'm speaking of food and sex analogously. The power of a person's sexual appetite is sometimes as powerful as a person's need for food. A more theological understanding of what it means for a couple to consummate the relationship is necessary. The relationship between food and faith has great impact on salvation history when a couple heeds God's mandate to be fruitful and multiply. A couple's paternal and pastoral responsibilities represent God's providential care by ensuring that each mouth is fed and each soul is nurtured. These descriptive food-faith analogies require deeper reflection in order to understand what role couples play in God's saving plan.

The *Catechism of the Catholic Church* explains there are two vocations that bring God's holiness and salvation into the world: the vocation to the priesthood and the faithful commitment of marriage (see *CCC*, 1534). People generally look to the clergy or religious, feeling that it is the responsibility of the "man of the cloth" and the "nun in the habit" to reveal God's plan for humanity. While this is true, it is also the responsibility and vocation of married couples. By looking at their vocation, using food-related terms, a couple can see how they are actually primarily responsible for fostering an attitude of holiness as part of God's salvific plan for the world. It is the domestic church, the home, where a child first develops a love for and understanding of God (see *Familiaris Consortio*, 21). This happens by the very act of Mom and Dad being fruitful and bringing life into the world. Every life conceived and every child welcomed into a loving family brings us closer to the reality envisioned by God's plan in salvation history.

You might be thinking, *Is he saying that simply having babies is part of God's plan for our salvation?* And my answer is "Yes!" Every life brought into this world in obedience to God's plan is an unveiling of salvation history before our eyes. Science tries to replace the conjugal act of man and woman, but God's plan qualifies that it's meant to be between husband and wife.

Science tries to redefine the roles of man and woman, especially regarding same-sex unions. But no one can argue that a child born into a loving home by a mother and father is a bad thing. According to the sacred Scripture, a mother and father for every child is intended by God; parents cooperate in a special way with God's saving history—one baby at a time! Loving parents that bring a child into this world are doing a good thing.

Bringing life into the world, however, depends on whether the husband and wife are following God's diet plan when it comes to their sexual activity. Is their sexual activity truly a generous act of self-giving, or is there a withholding of the seed, or a determination to deny the egg to be fertilized? Do they hunger for each other in a wholesome and holy way that is intentionally open to life, or does their sexual act simply satisfy their urges and cravings? Do they see each other's fruitfulness and sexual love for each other as a gift they freely give to each other or a right to be demanded of each other? Do they see fruitfulness and potency as threats requiring protection?

The understanding of human and conjugal sexuality between husband and wife, when it's seen as a gift, respects physical intimacy and treats the other person with kindness and charity—much like the way one approaches a fine meal. Conversely, when sexuality is demanded as a right, this cheapens it, and people take it in without care, similar to the way they approach fast food. It becomes merely the biological act of eating rather than a sophisticated, mature act of celebration.

Couples might regularly ask themselves whether they are practicing the virtue of moderation when it comes to their sexual appetites. As in the case of dietary regulations, one can become easily addicted to certain foods when abused. If there is no discipline when it comes to seeking sexual pleasure, a couple can become gluttonous, full of lustful cravings. Sexual addiction can only be mastered when it follows a prescription for when and with whom sexual activity can be shared. This understanding reveals God's saving plan for couples—and for the world. He did not make us to wantonly participate in orgies, bestiality, or abuse. No, out of his love for us, God created us to love.

Spouses' Mutual Responsibility: Fulfilling the Hunger

On a more intimate food and faith-related topic, couples must be willing to consider whether their love for each other satisfies each other's cravings for intimacy, lest one goes elsewhere to be satisfied. In the case of Eve, had Adam truly provided for her, would it have been as easy for the devil to persuade her? Spouses require more honest conversation with each other regarding their own sexual cravings and the mutual responsibility they share in satisfying each other. Without this, it is very likely that one or both of the spouses will be tempted to look elsewhere and satisfy their cravings. The alarming rate of infidelity, one-night stands, and casual sexual relationships is on the rise, and unfortunately this is very much accepted as normal in our modern day. Equally alarming and parallel to our topic is how an unhealthy diet is celebrated as a norm, and fast food all too often now replaces the family meal. Normalizing the bad and scorning the good demonstrates how far we've wandered from the path of truth and salvation's history. It shows that we have become what we eat—lies, half-truths, and more forbidden fruits—on a regular basis.

Both acts of eating and sexual expression are biological realities required for the sustenance of the human race. On one hand, some are called to a life of discipline without sexual expression, and some share a similar discipline regarding food intake through rigorous forms of fasting. While these acts are certainly biological, they are not limited only to the body. Both sexuality and food affect the totality of the human person. Both affect the mind, heart, and soul as well. Sexuality and what one eats both affect one's psychology. In fact, hunger and cravings begin in the mind. With the amount of psychological junk food that is being thrown at our young people every day through suggestive advertising, semi-pornographic forms of entertainment, and blatant sexual activity available on the Internet, it's easy to understand why the psychosexual development of young people is not only hindered but disordered or even destroyed. Society needs to reconsider how the mind is being fed, especially when it comes to difficult and sensitive topics regarding human sexuality. If not, we will develop into a very unholy nation, far from God's saving plan in history.

At the same time, there is a particular way that food and sexuality uniquely influence the rational soul. Consider how, from a positive perspective, both food and sex can bring comfort to a person. When abused, both can bring anxiety and pain. Saying that sexual activity is primarily or exclusively a biological act of survival would turn us into irrational animals running around in the jungle, doing anything we can to survive—including eating our own. Like food, sexuality touches upon the affections and properties of the rational soul. It forms the identity of a person and determines one's character. Consider a slovenly person who eats poorly and without care. That person's identity is formed as unhealthy, and even gross. The same is true for those who have no discernment in the sexual act—they do it and they don't really care; it simply satisfies a biological urge. Those people become just as unhealthy and gross, acting more like a dog in heat that tries to copulate with the leg of a chair. Without any discernment of how sexuality affects the soul, we have become a people attached to the sexual act without meaning, and in a sense, we have lost our souls. And at the very least, we have lost our way on the path that leads to salvation.

Prior to the Fall, sexuality and food were understood positively. Food was plentiful. Sexuality was not something to be ashamed of, evidenced by Adam and Eve's unselfconscious nudity. After the Fall, however, these two biological realities—human sexuality and human physical sustenance through food—take on a more confused, imbalanced, and even negative role in the lives of God's people. They no longer have free access to food; they cover their nakedness in shame. Something went very wrong for this once-innocent couple, all because they partook of the forbidden fruit.

Food and Sexual Revolution and Redemption

But God knows that his plan for salvation will involve redeeming humanity by redeeming both food and sex. God wants to bring about a balance of understanding and expression. When done rightly, all is good in the world. When done wrongly, so goes the direction of salvation history. When there is a godly approach to both food and sexuality in the life of God's people—and in particular married couples—there is harmony and we see a glimpse of the Garden of Eden, and we begin to trust that God will provide.

However, the devil knows that our appetites are easily distorted. With eyes bigger than our stomachs, it is easy for the devil to tempt humanity with imbalanced cravings—a combination of lust and gluttony—that work together to obtain more of everything (including more sex, more food) as a symbol of a godly equality. The desire to store up treasures on earth—whether that means excessive grain bins or boasting about how many people you can get to fall in love with you—is a common temptation. More food or more sex can make a person feel superior—even slightly omnipotent (powerful), omnibenevolent (beloved), and omniscient (smart), which are the three properties of God, not man. Gaining accessibility to unlimited food (security) and sex (pleasure) can make a person feel happy, especially those with a disordered appetite and a feebly formed conscience.

On the contrary, God never meant satisfaction to be achieved in this world; satisfaction is reserved only for those who are willing to suffer hunger for the sake of the world to come, where all our hungers will be satisfied. Of course, the devil doesn't want us to believe that heaven is real, which is why so many people work so hard to make this world their own personal heaven, filled with endless food and unlimited sex.

While some may think this thesis about food and faith and

couples is a stretch, consider what happens when many young couples are encouraged to consider Church teaching regarding the immorality of contraception. When they are reminded to practice the virtue of abstinence prior to marriage (and even at particular times during marriage), many couples become slightly hostile, or at least defensive, when faced with the idea that somehow God, or the Church, or some priest, is denying them this pleasure. Some actually feel that not engaging in sexual act would be impossible and detrimental to their relationship. That's why contraception continues to be a popular, multibillion-dollar product for sexually active and sex hungry people—people want the sex, but they don't want the baby. They want to till the land, but not actually plant the seed. They want to consume the food, but they don't want to swallow and digest it; instead they want to regurgitate it. These are harsh but indicative food and sex analogies.

The idea that sex and food are rights puts men and women in the unique position to take control of these activities. This includes controlling when to bring children into the world, which is ultimately God's prerogative but something in which man and woman are called to participate. Science can already make food grow outside of the proper season. In the same way, science can grow children outside of the sexual act, and it can deny a child life, even when it is a fertile time for the mother.

Whether or not it's a good thing to grow food out of season is an ongoing debate. Local organic farmers protest genetic modification that makes foods grow year-round and the scientific techniques used to manipulate food unnaturally have a negative impact on the human diet. Having access to certain foods year-round is an example of how humanity has become somewhat spoiled. We have become addicted to immediately gratifying our cravings, rather than waiting for the proper seasons to celebrate. We falsely believe that our humongous storage bins will provide for a lifetime, and we forget the One who promised to provide eternally (see Matthew 6:19). At the same time, it makes us seem independent, making us less dependent on God's providence. The ability to grow food (or a baby!) in a test tube has distorted God's plan for us. We have become our own gods. The original temptation in the Garden of Eden continues in our land of plenty!

The connection between food, faith, and a couple's responsibility can be further described in agricultural terms—either natural or unnatural. With pills that increase potency for men and other pills that inhibit fertility in women, couples begin to satisfy their sexual cravings *unnaturally*, whether they are married or not. This control puts them on par—or at least lets them *think* they are on par—with God's ability to bring forth life or deny it in this world.

However, when a couple humbly submits to God's plan and views their sexuality (and their craving for sex) as a gift that they must approach with sobriety and full responsibility, they begin to cooperate with God's plan for their lives. They also enter more deeply into the history of salvation, of which married couples are intimately a part. They begin to recognize that each sexual act is a part of God's plan to share their love with each other. They have a responsibility to learn about each other and respect the natural cycle of their own fruitfulness. When they are able to bring children into this world, they freely and responsibly nourish their children, thus fulfilling God's desire for them.

DEALING WITH THE DEVIL'S DESTRUCTIVE DIET

In order to cooperate with God's plan and overcome the devil's temptations, a couple needs insight into how the devil operates. What's the devil's game plan for destroying a couple's unity? A family's communal life? Society's soul? How can a couple continue on a proper path toward salvation?

Fortunately, the Church has always been aware of the devil's unoriginal plan. The approach used to tempt couples in today's world is very similar to the technique used to tempt Adam and Eve. The devil makes something that is bad for us look good—good enough to eat. When we take a bite—a symbol of accepting something internally, intimately, and personally into ourselves—the devil wins, at least that particular battle. The act of putting something in your mouth, whether it's food or putting another person's lips so close to your own, is an extremely intimate act. Eating, which can be understood as oral intimacy, requires trust, acceptance, and love. Just ask your kids! If they don't want to eat something, or if they don't trust what you want to feed them, they will let you know with their mouths shut tight. But if your kids know you, love you, and want to share joy with you, they will kiss you with sweetness beyond compare! In a sense, this is what the devil wants to do by gaining our trust, our confidence, and our intimacy. This is why we teach our children, "Don't accept candy from strangers!"

The devil wants us to take a bite of the forbidden. Like Judas's kiss, the devil wants to be as close to our lips without really loving us. (And we know the irreparable harm that kiss did to the One who saves history.)

Our oral fixation, closely connected to the faithful spouses showing love for each other by kissing and our desire to live by eating, began when we were children. A child's innocence and the desire to learn about everything means that everything makes its way into the child's mouth. The intimacy of putting things into our mouths is a part of a child's learning process. Unless well-guarded, the child could easily put something harmful into his or her mouth. The devil knows this, which is why the food and faith analogy is helpful for couples to consider. God is still telling us—in particular married couples—that to eat the forbidden fruit out of a selfish desire will eventually create enmity between us.

PILLS OF POWER

For Men

Couples are often tempted to put something else into their mouths that affects their relationship to God and each other: Viagra. Medications for erectile dysfunction are popularly understood to boost potency and prove virility. It makes older men feel young again, a veritable fountain of youth—which, by the way, doesn't exist except in storybook fantasies. While these pills can be used to create appropriate levels of intimacy within marriage, it is also abused by men who hunger for ongoing sexual satisfaction, often without the consequence of a child.

One small bite can make a man potent—and, in the minds of some, always potent. This sounds very similar to the "omnipotency" of God, something that the first commandment warns us not to seek lest we find ourselves arrogantly competing against God and not humbly accepting the natural slowing down of sexual activity that comes with age. It only makes sense that the male biology would not be able to sexually perform at an older age, simply because naturally, a man would not have the energy to provide and care for the children that could come from the sexual activity. (Of course, men who use this pill can be easily deluded into thinking they are stronger than they really are.)

Taking a male enhancement pill is not a sin in and of itself. It could be used to bring his wife satisfaction—a good and noble thing. However, when abused and when used outside of God's plan, it can bring about an unhealthy and unrealistic understanding of the sexual act, as evidenced by the growing number of sexually transmitted diseases in the older male population—many senior citizens and widowers. Men who use this pill should approach the sexual act with humility.

For Women

On the other hand, the birth control pill gives women a unique power—the power to decide if and when to bring life into the world. This pill has convinced women that they can control their own fruitfulness and life-giving ability. It provides for the tilling of the field, but not for planting the seed in the soil. Birth control is contrary to salvation history's desire to people the earth, to be fruitful and multiply. The pill can cause a naturally fecund woman to become barren—a curse in sacred Scripture (see Exodus 23). Strangely, the pill for men makes what is naturally weakened unnaturally hyper-functional, while for a woman, the pill unnaturally breaks something that was naturally functioning—her fertility. Through the intervention of science and technology (but with a resistance to theology), men and women enter into sexual relationships without true intimacy, because the fertility and virility are literally on different pages. They want to touch physically, but avoid each other interiorly.

As said before, there may be some legitimate reasons for the use of the pill in appropriate and unique marital situations, such as a husband who wants to be a father or a woman struggling with an irregular menstrual cycle or a condition such as endometriosis. However, for the most part, the use of these pills is motivated by selfishness, a disregard for God's natural plan, and a fear-filled appetite for sexual satisfaction. The desire for sexual activity, an ever-growing appetite in the modern world, is as addictive as certain foods or drink, and it's often hormonally grown or chemically filled. While the Church's theology has matured in speaking about sexual activity between married couples as being a "good," it is always clarified with words or phrases such as "moderation," "never abusing the gift," and making sure the sexual activity "respects and humbly submits to the natural cycles of fruitfulness"—the same humility as a farmer who must obey nature, cultivating the land at the right place and time (see CCC, 1809, 2512, 2522, and 2405).

Sexual activity outside the marriage covenant is always considered a forbidden fruit. But the devil's ability to make these bite-sized "pills of power" so attractive has led to a gluttonous approach toward sexual satisfaction, a disordered appetite, and an unabashed desire to consume the forbidden fruit in season and out of season. Satisfying sexual cravings, so widely accepted, has led to destructive repercussions. The results of this unchecked sexual hunger can easily be tied to legalized abortion, post-abortive trauma, child sexual abuse, the spread of sexually transmitted diseases, normalization of sexual perversion, sexual and gender confusion, and ultimately being isolated from God's fruitful, faithful, and loving plan for humanity. On a basic level, these easily consumed sins prevent people from sharing in the banquet on earth—and sadly, if unconfessed, eventually the eternal banquet of heaven.

A Bigger Banquet for the Definition of Love

Couples that cooperate with God's plan for salvation recognize the power of moderating their sexual appetites, practice a bigger definition of love—one that is not limited to sexual activity—and ultimately become more open to God's plan. They may even actively invite God's presence in the midst of their intimacy, helping each other to grow in virtue. Many couples trust that God will be a part of their sexual activity, asking him to guarantee that they are actually making love and not just having sex. This is the same trust that farmers must have when they plant their crops. They must cooperate with nature, collaborate with God, and pray and trust that God will provide enough to eat, even if there is another mouth to feed. Couples ought to use this same earthy spirituality when they feel the urge to share love with each other.

Without a developed sense of faith and their role in salvation history, couples will be tempted to satisfy their lower sexual appetites, like a spoiled overweight child who throws a temper tantrum at the slightest sign of hunger. It will be easy to break God's commandment regarding fidelity to each other, and it can tempt individuals to covet the possessions of the neighbor (whether a product or a person). This temptation sparked King David's desire for Bathsheba, a married woman. David even used food and drink to tempt her husband Uriah—enticing him with rich and fatty foods and getting him drunk with wine, and then abandoning him in the heat of the battle, which resulted in his death. As previously noted, David's gluttonous lust had a serious effect on salvation history; his actions required a serious period of fasting and mourning (see 2 Samuel 11).

David angered God again by taking a census of the people, which could be interpreted as David playing God by actions that would lead either to population control or forcibly trying to increase numbers for his own military power. David's attempts to control or manipulate life were no different from what modern nations now do through forced abortions or incentives to make babies. David's sin was presumption: the idea that he could manipulate the Holy Spirit, the Lord and Giver of Life. David's prescribed punishment (a choice of poisons), affected the well-being of his people as well as his kingly ability to feed the flock entrusted to his care (see 2 Samuel 24).

THE ETERNAL WEDDING BANQUET

Jesus, on the other hand, was the ultimate example of obedience to God's plan, a perfect model for married couples. He manifested his power with food at the wedding feast of Cana. His final days on earth celebrated the unique food of the Passover covenant, a supper that showed how God is wedded to his people. He spoke about the consummation of all salvation history as an invitation to a wedding banquet.

These food and faith images, particularly those that evoke spousal fidelity, show God's plan to have all of humanity joined together in the celebration of the eternal wedding banquet. Furthermore, God wants to enter into that intimate union with each person *exclusively*, as a lover seeks the beloved. In the Eucharist, God—who hungers for us—wants us to develop a hunger for communion with him. Whenever we receive the Eucharist, he is intimately placed on our tongues as a foretaste of the heavenly feast.

The high point of the Mass is called the consummation; this occurs when the priest receives the Body and Blood of Christ in the sacred liturgy. In some liturgies, the altar server rings a bell at that point of Holy Communion. At the same time, the highest point of married love is manifested in the consummation of a couples' love for each other—represented by the wedding bells at Church. The marriage act joins the two in the most intimate communion—a holy communion. In both the sacrament of marriage and the priesthood, the love of the spouse becomes food for the other.

Continuing this analogy, something powerful happens when two lovers give themselves to each other completely. Couples who do not put anything between their love by using contraception cooperate with God's plan of salvation in a powerfully unique way. Couples that give themselves totally to each other bear the fruit of their love. Their self-giving actually brings about the potentiality of new life, an incarnation of their love. The pregnancy of a faithful couple fulfills an important role in salvation history. In a more biblical sense, the couple participates in peopling the earth—and, God willing, peopling heaven.

The collaboration between spouses to bring life into the world reflects God's power. Their cooperation in feeding the child from the womb and ensuring that the child will eventually learn how to feed himself demonstrates parents who are truly reflecting the image of God for their children. As God feeds his children, so parents feed their children in God's name. Feeding a child from the womb and then feeding them the Bread and Wine that will bring them to the heavenly banquet propels humanity closer to the goal of salvation history. Holy marriages provide an example, a true witness of God, and helps others return to God's original plan. When couples continue to work with God in their marriages by feeding each other, nourishing their children, cooperating with the natural laws of biological reproduction, and moderating their sexual appetites, they experience a type of divine union with God. They realize that God fulfills every hope and desire—not just for their marriage but for the eternal union of the never-ending love at the marriage feast in heaven.

SOMETHING TO CHEW ON

There is an ongoing debate about what the forbidden fruit looked like. While it is usually represented as an apple, others suggest that it was a pomegranate. No one will ever know, nor does it matter. However, couples can and should discuss what the forbidden fruits in their relationship are. For example, they can consider some of the things a spouse should never do, lest it negatively impact the couple's relationship in grave ways. At the same time, a couple's love for each other imitates the love between Christ and his Church—a love that is always forgiving! Couples are encouraged to share a meal (perhaps a dessert) using passion fruit to be cooked, served, and eaten when they have had a disagreement, struggle, or fight and have reconciled. This can serve as a very solid reminder that even though one or the other has eaten a forbidden fruit, they are determined to be reconciled to each other, and then celebrate their reconciliation with a delicious dessert—hardly a forbidden food. In order to live the sacrament of marriage, they can share a special meal together to remind them of this reconciliation. Just as the Eucharist represents the fatted calf prepared for the Prodigal Son, what special meal could signify true forgiveness between spouses?

PRACTICAL THEOLOGY FOR THE DINNER TABLE

1. How can a married couple take a more active role in salvation history?
2. How can a regular meal strengthen a couple's relationship with each other and God?

3. How can a disordered appetite among spouses negatively affect their marriage?

4. Why do you think God uses the image of a wedding banquet to describe heaven?

5. Are children seen as a blessing or as a curse in the modern world? How does this attitude affect salvation history?

CHAPTER SIX

Feeding the Hungry— Body, Mind, and Spirit

There was a rich man, who was clothed in purple and fine linen and who feasted sumptuously each day. And at his gate lay a poor man named Lazarus, full of sores, who desired to be fed with what fell from the rich man's table; moreover, the dogs came and licked his sores. The poor man died and was carried by the angels to Abraham's bosom. The rich man also died and was buried; and in Hades, being in torment, he lifted up his eyes and saw Abraham far off and Lazarus in his bosom. And he called out, "Father Abraham, have mercy on me, and send Lazarus to dip the end of his finger in water and cool my tongue, for I am in anguish in this flame." Abraham said, 'Son, remember that you in your lifetime received your good things, and Lazarus in like manner evil things; but now he is comforted here, and you are in anguish." (Luke 16:19–25)

God's original plan was to sustain his children physically here on earth and guide them and keep them safe spiritually as they journey to eternal life. Jesus continued this saving act in his own life, and it continues today through the mission of the Church, the sacred nature of the priesthood, and the lofty vocation of marriage. But what about those who remain hungry?

Are these poor souls somehow excluded by God's plan of salvation? Or are the children who have feasted on God's goodness somehow failing to continue this course of salvation history through sins of omission? Each living person on earth has a role to play in God's saving action. We participate in salvation history when we collaborate with God in fulfilling his original plan: to feed those who hunger in body, mind, and spirit.

It's easy to forget the basics of faith—the corporal works of mercy: feeding the hungry and giving water to the thirsty (see Matthew 25:31–46). In our efforts to reach the heights of the spiritual life, we have to remind those with their heads in the clouds not to trip on the homeless and hungry person on the street corner. Before we're meant to understand the profound teachings regarding the Eucharist as the super-substantial food, God provides a practical theology of food to prepare us for it. Food, feeding people, and being fed are essential human experiences that shape our spiritual ones.

APPETIZING SIGNS OF GOD'S LOVE AND CARE

During a retreat at the seminary, the retreat leader asked us to eat our meals in silence. She asked us to chew slowly and meditate on the origins of the food. We were to recall and consider, as best we could, the process of how the food got to the point that it was now on our plates, ready for our enjoyment and sustenance. It was quite a humbling exercise to consider how many people were involved in the process of each bite I took. The meal was truly the fruit of the earth and "work of human hands," but it first began with God. Food, initiated by God as the sure sign of his love and care, is what motivates the Catholic Church's mission to feed the hungry and poor. In keeping with the Lord's command, the Church proves her holiness and obedience to God every time we perform the corporal works of mercy: feeding the hungry, giving drink to the thirsty, clothing the naked, sheltering the homeless, comforting the sick, visiting prisoners, and burying the dead. These are the basics of human life that *must* be done in order to get to the next level that we hope will get us to heaven. If not, salvation history takes an unfortunate turn for those who seek it.

These corporal works of mercy, which complement the spiritual works of mercy, show how God pays just as much attention to our humanity as he does to our spirituality. He sees the importance, and even necessity, of caring for bodily needs. After all, he made the human body through his life-giving breath and redeemed it through his Son's sacrifice on the cross. We are composed of a harmonious balance of the body, mind, and spirit; therefore, a balanced and harmonious approach to our being re-rooted in salvation history requires paying attention to our body, mind, and spirit at the same time. Our bodies will experience decay in death, while our spirits will live forever in heaven, but we are also reminded that our bodies will experience a resurrection—a perfection—on the last day. In other words, it's important to pay attention to how the body and soul are supposed to work together, even through our broken human nature. That was God's original plan. Wouldn't it be a type of heaven if our will and actions, our mind and heart, and our soul and body agreed and worked with each other? This beautiful harmony of will and action, body and spirit, *was* Adam and Eve's original situation prior to the Fall. After the Fall, the war between body and soul began, and it rages on in all of us.

WE ARE ALL CONNECTED

How can we try to recapture a sense of harmony between the body and soul? The answer is seen in the way Jesus perfectly fulfilled God's saving plan. Jesus cared for the broken, hurting parts of the body of Christ. By establishing a theological understanding of the body of Christ as consisting of many parts, all connected, Jesus taught us that the only way to have harmony in our own individual lives is to recognize how we are all connected. If one of us hurts, we all hurt. If one member cries out in need, but we are deaf to his or her pleas, instead of harmony, there is only cacophony.

Jesus taught us that feeding the poor, caring for the sick, and providing the basics to those most in need has a remedial effect on our own personal brokenness. Social justice—not to be confused with political actions motivated by religious agendas—is part of the mission of the Church. Social justice, understood theologically, helps a person to become a saint! And between now and the time the person gets to heaven, it actually brings about more balance between the body of Christ's hurting and non-hurting members.

While it is necessary to feed the soul with the *Catechism* and the Church's teachings and sacred traditions, we should remember that, at its core, theology is the combination of mystical and ascetical practices. In other words, it's not enough to just pray and study; it's just as important to get out there and prove one's faith by serving the poor, caring for the sick, and so on (see James 2:14–26). Theology is summarized in pastoral activity!

SEEING CHRIST IN THOSE WE SERVE

While an atheist can do social justice and corporal works of mercy to care for the needs of the poor, the Christian does this work because they are ultimately and actually caring for Jesus Christ, whose presence is stamped in humanity's brokenness, and more importantly, in human dignity. "As you did it to one of the least of these my brethren, you did it to me" (Matthew 25:40). A Christian doing social justice isn't doing it just for the sake of being kind. He's doing it because he sees Christ in the other person. He's not merely serving humanity; he's serving others in order to better understand the call to divinity. The difference between a believer and a really kind humanist is that the Christian understands that the person being served is Christ himself, revealed and present in the lives of the poor. Christians serve the poor because they know Jesus, and they recognize him in the poor. They recognize that Jesus made himself poor, unrecognized by many who called themselves religious leaders, but very apparent to those who had a heartfelt love and belief in God's compassion—people like the first shepherds, those he healed, and of course his most intimate followers. An atheist does not recognize Jesus in the poor. Instead, the atheist sees himself as a type of messiah who helps the poor out of their plight. The difference is measured by the caregiver's knowledge and love of the person of Jesus. For those who believe, it is Jesus they serve, and it is Jesus who serves the poor through, with, and in them.

Both/And, Not Either/Or

Unfortunately, tensions arise in the Catholic Church between those who are more spiritually inclined and those who are more social justice-oriented. A good theological analysis of this tension will always reveal the need for both approaches to the faith. From a theological and pastoral perspective, sound Catholic theology doesn't employ an "either/or" approach, but rather a "both/and" approach. We need both in order to be truly good Christians. When we forget to balance academic work with pastoral activity, or the spiritual life with our human life, we tend to approach God's path for us from a skewed direction. Yet, even though we have very skewed vision and tendencies that try to pull us to the left or the right, we must always regroup, seek balance, and try to walk the straight path.

The one thing that has always brought the Church back to the faith's foundation is service to the poor—particularly feeding the hungry. Yes, *food* becomes the instrument through which we can correct our faults and failures. Consider St. Peter's threefold requirement to prove he loves Jesus: "Feed my flock!" (see John 21:15–17).

Over the two-thousand-year tradition of the Catholic Church, many men and women have been raised up to the great dignity and the title of saints in heaven. These were holy men and women who had a highly developed theology of the Eucharist and an equally developed theology of food. Consider how the simple act of feeding people—Christians and pagans alike—helped Teresa of Calcutta to become one of the modern world's most impressive, powerful, and influential women. Mother Teresa of

Calcutta follows a long tradition of saints who recognized the eternal value of giving one bite to the hungry or a sip of water to the thirsty. This is exactly what God did for Adam, Eve, and all the rest of the human family he seeks to save.

Feeding anyone who is hungry—poor and rich alike—with the same compassion as if we were feeding Christ himself can help all of us (mothers, teachers, cafeteria workers, cooks, and dads who like to grill) to become saints. If we try to serve the poor and hungry as Jesus would feed them—providing sustenance for their bodies but also nourishment for their souls—then we can become holy members of God's army, fighting against the forces that seek to deprive life. We become integral members in the role of salvation's history, of which Jesus is the author, origin, and the destined goal.

REGROUPING AND REBALANCING

The Church's patrimony will always be under suspicion by people who don't want to believe in the one true Church founded by Jesus Christ. However, Church critics (or in some cases enemies) cannot dispute its demonstration of motherly love when feeding the poor. As one of the longest lasting institutions in world history, the Catholic Church has proudly proclaimed a compassion for the poor—not motivated by pity but by the faith that such loving service brings us closer to salvation history's goal. When the Church forgets this mission, it becomes an easy target for critics who see it as an institution only interested in finances, committees, covering up scandals, and bureaucracy.

Throughout history, Christians have struggled to maintain the correct balance between theology and action. St. Francis Xavier and St. Damien of Molokai both wrestled with being faced with so many pastoral needs while too many priests were locked away in the ivory tower of academics, thus missing the opportunity to really exercise their fatherly role by feeding God's children. Missionaries who were sent to new and strange lands had to develop a trusting relationship with the indigenous people by providing food, companionship, and collaboration *before* they could catechize successfully. Soup kitchens are a modern-day example. These are often sponsored by faithful believers who demonstrate their theology by simply providing food and companionship to the hungry and homeless. Finally, consider how today's young people in the Church are reminded to live a more balanced life by distributing Christmas food baskets to the poor. There is nothing more jolting—in a good way—than giving a hungry person something to eat.

A Mind-Set of Generosity

While it is easy to talk about feeding the poor, actually doing so requires a theological mind-set and Christian generosity. The world's starving population is an unfortunate reality because it's actually not necessary. It seems to me that there is certainly enough food in the world to feed hungry people everywhere. What's missing is the *generosity*—not in actual monetary donations but in the selfless act of dedicating oneself to organize systems that create a flow for the food donations to actually reach those in need. I've met with various food donation centers, and they've shared this same concern with me. They have food to give, but something seems to block the way to actually get the food to those who desperately need it.

Feeding the poor also requires lawmakers, politicians, and others in the public service sector to create laws and policies based on a generous spirit (rather than legal ramifications) in order to provide tangible aid. Too often, laws require jumping through endless hoops just to get food in the mouths of the poor. Seemingly endless legalities and red tape deter many good-hearted, well-intentioned people from getting more involved for fear of the old adage: "No good deed goes unpunished." Jesus himself was certainly punished for healing the sick (see Luke 13:14), feeding his disciples (see Mark 2:23), and telling the truth about the ungodly red tape that legally minded religious leaders created (see Matthew 23:4).

We face tremendous battles in the spiritual realm. The way to counteract the attacks from the Church's enemies is to do what Mother Church does best: feed the poor children of God as the body of Christ! While worldly minded members of society criticize the Church and her members for what they perceive as inconsistencies regarding faith, they cannot deny the power of faith when it comes to loving the poor as Jesus loved us.

Another important aspect of feeding the hungry is an understanding of *who* is actually hungry. The keen observer of Christian doctrine will recognize that the sacramental Eucharistic hospitality given only to Catholics does not preclude sharing a meal with those who cannot receive the Eucharist. Faithful Catholics should have no trouble sharing a meal with sinners, especially since Jesus did the same. St. Paul admonished St. Peter when he noticed some division at the dinner table, as St. Peter separated himself from the Gentiles (foreigners and uncircumcised). The theology of food can be shared by all humanity, even though the theology of the Eucharist is not understood and therefore celebrated by people of different faiths. While we cannot extend Eucharistic hospitality to just *anyone*, Mother Church's children can still eat with *everyone*! We can still offer non-communicants something to eat and celebrate a form of thanksgiving, in hopes that we might one day celebrate the sacrament of thanksgiving in the Eucharist.

A Puritan's Diet or Pastoral Charity?

I recall the experience of eating a meal with other food bloggers, a unique gathering of people. While some were very surprised to see a priest there, others recognized me from some of my food work on TV. At one point, a same-sex couple began asking me questions about Church doctrine, especially regarding moral practices. You can imagine how challenging it was to share a meal with people who held views so different from my own. I prayed, asking Jesus to help me to see him in myself and in others (remembering that they are still children of God). At the end of our conversation—at times heated but always respectful and always directed to appreciating one another's existence— this couple told me that they experienced a sort of conversion. They said, "Our dinner with you makes us hate the Church less." I saw this as a victory—a step in the right direction of salvation history. I've often reflected on how this meal, the dinner conversation, and the understanding that we all have something in common—namely the fact that we all need to eat— became a moment to practice that challenging balance between theological orthodoxy, avoiding a puritanical approach to faith, and the activity of pastoral charity.

While I didn't win that couple over to be immediately baptized, there was a sacramental moment when I was reminded that Jesus did something similar. He ate with sinners. Being a sinner myself, I recognized the need for pastoral humility when eating with those who may be publicly sinning, because I may be *privately* sinning—which is just as offensive in God's eyes!

Jesus's dinner encounters with sinners—prostitutes and tax collectors—usually ended up with powerful conversion experiences for the former sinner and future saint. I'm not God. But the very fact that I was willing to eat with those who consider the Church an enemy showed that I was open to this technique of balancing pastoral charity with my theological training. I need more practice in serving people God's saving message of Good News!

Feeding people who cannot pay us back—or who want to pay us back with an insult—can be considered a pastoral and sacramental opportunity. It's pastoral because the sheep cannot repay the shepherd. It's sacramental because it reminds us of the sacred: the fact that God is present when sin abounds, light is needed when encountering the darkness, and we are called to be salt of the earth because we bring spice to life and act as the saline agent to cleanse and cure! The simple act of feeding people can be an authentic healing act, because it's deeply connected to the exercise of hospitality. Just as the hospital is the place of healing, the act of hospitality can cure many ills.

A Good and Noble Gathering

Many times I've wondered if a theologically understood social justice moment could include an ecumenical and interreligious dinner. The only agenda would be eating together. It would certainly be a unique experience to have leaders from different (and at times warring) religions to come together for the simple purpose of sharing a meal. No one would try to solve key differences and theological concerns; instead, it would merely be a reminder of humanity's common need for fellowship and food. While individuals might disagree on key issues, such a dinner would prove that they have the most basic thing in common: We are human. We are God's children. What would it take for such a good and noble gathering? It seems that we would need to hunger for it, and have the keen sensibility to detect who is hungry in the world. I believe and have seen that the Church, through her ecumenical and interreligious efforts, is very hungry for world peace and religious harmony! Our loving God wants to feed us all.

Feeding the Rich and Famous

What about feeding those who have it all? In other words, does the theologically influenced social justice act of feeding people extend to those who are rich, powerful, and famous? The saintly Teresa of Calcutta, speaking at a powerful gathering of leaders in Washington, DC, spoke of America as a rich country, yet one of the poorest countries in the world. With the richness of her personal faith and the poverty from her vows well lived, Mother Teresa taught another important social justice concern.

She pointed out that some of the rich, powerful, and famous are actually *starving* for faith, hope, and love.

While it can hardly be considered a rigorous missionary effort to evangelize the wealthy, the rich are in need of experts who can feed their faith. Those with deep pockets or powerful positions are sometimes the most difficult people to feed because they seem to have it all. Jesus's encounter with the rich young man (see Mark 10:17–31) reminds us how both the shallow soil and the soil filled with weeds make it very difficult to evangelize—to plant the Word of God in a way that will bear fruit.

In food terms, charity to the poor requires not only giving someone a fish, but teaching that person *how* to fish. The knowledge and training that comes from theologically understood social justice programs give food and also *dignity* that comes when God's capable children manifest their potential. However, when it comes to feeding the rich, special attention is needed to hear the deeper cries and longing underneath the surface of glamour, beauty, and popularity. It's amazing—and at the same time sad—to discover that popular Hollywood actors, superstar athletes, top-of-the-charts musicians, and powerful political leaders have such interior brokenness hidden deeply behind an attractive and powerful exterior. While there are not enough shepherds who can feed the poor, there are even fewer shepherds who can guide the rich and famous. But do they not need just as much, if not more guidance, as the poor? Or do we think that they, by their monetary value, somehow need God less?

In her efforts to feed the poor, the Church must consider opportunities to reach out in a special way to those who have many material possessions. The wealthy are starving for meaning in their lives, and it cannot come from their possessions. The rich young man who Jesus encountered in the Scriptures faced the same challenge. He had much, he followed all of the commands, but he wasn't willing to make a radical change and give it all away to the poor. This passage requires a literal and allegorical understanding of Jesus's command. Jesus was asking him to become one of his intimate disciples, someone who would give everything up for his sake.

Prudence Prevails

While all are called to discipleship, there are degrees to which people are called, and therefore, varying degrees of giving up personal possessions. If you have a family, you cannot recklessly give everything to the poor while your own family starves. That would be a violation of your response to God's call, and it would just be plain ignorance of God's providence.

In considering this command to give all away in order to have the greatest treasure in heaven, common sense must prevail, aided by a prudent understanding of practical finances. The virtue of humility helps to engage the process so that those with financial needs can make distinctions between wants and needs. We need experts, in our churches and in our communities, to help guide us in making theologically influenced financial decisions. I'm not suggesting that we pray for God to tell us what stock we ought to invest in, but we must ask God to give us the proper perspective regarding giving to the poor, making donations to the Church, and providing financial stability for our families. When was the last time your family prayed together about how to spend your money? When was the last time you had a frank discussion with other family members about how you could serve the poor, or how much to put in the church's poor box?

DIRECT INVOLVEMENT WITH THE POOR

For those who do have a lot of money, pastors can nourish their spiritual lives by providing opportunities for the rich to get *directly* and *personally* involved in feeding the poor. When a pastor approaches a person with money, he often forgets to feed them spiritually. While his objective is to generally get a bigger donation for the Church or a special project, how much more effective would it be if he invited the wealthy person to participate in a feeding-the-hungry or serving-the-poor program? A rich person can easily give money, which would certainly be appreciated. But if wealthy people could also donate some of their time and physical presence in ministering to those in need, it would be an even greater investment. The experience of working with the poor and feeding the hungry often stirs up the Holy Spirit to *increase* the virtue of charity in the soul who has so much. This results in an active participation and collaboration in the corporal works of mercy.

Our Church's history is full of remarkable people who have experienced the richness of God on top of the material richness they have gained from financial success. St. Edward, St. Louis of France, St. Hedwig, St. Margaret of Scotland, St. Francis of Assisi, St. Claire of Assisi, St. Catherine of Sienna, St. Katherine

Drexel, and Blessed Pierre Giorgio Frassati are all saints who teach us that, despite possessing material goods, we could be missing the greatest treasure of all: faith, hope, and love. By being aware of this hunger in the lives of rich people (which these saints satisfied by serving the poor), the Church invites them to give not just money, but *themselves* in the act of serving the poor and hungry. This invitation for direct involvement provides the wealthy with a powerful perspective on humanity. They realize firsthand that money and possessions, while important and useful, do not define them. It enables them to build character and life-giving virtue. It roots them into recognizing how they are actively (and not just financially) members of the body of Christ.

Having the wealthy feed the poor brings about a just society. It generates respect and appreciation for each other's abilities as well as struggles. However, this is not an easy message to preach in a world that is becoming more and more self-centered, and at the same time divided as the body of Christ.

Forming Culture—One Family at a Time

The Church, as a loving mother, directs the world and forms culture with a view toward salvation. As part of this mission, the Church develops a preferential option for the poor—a recognition of who the poor are and why we serve them as a response to the commandments of Christ. This is done as part of the individual Christian's formation. While parish leaders catechize and prepare people at different ages and stages of maturity for the sacramental life of the Church, it's also very important to ensure that candidates preparing for each sacrament have some awareness about how feeding people is part of their sacramental responsibilities. Aided by the grace that comes from the proper reception of the Eucharist itself, recipients don't just receive Jesus—they become more like him.

May I suggest that an effective place for this awareness to develop would be as part of marriage preparation for young couples. As mentioned in the last chapter, married couples, by their virtue of the consummation of their love, have an intimate relationship with the theology of food. The priesthood and marriage are considered the two vocations that bring about God's holiness and justice in the world. But while it takes a man preparing for the priesthood six or more years to get ordained, there are very few requirements in comparison for a couple preparing for marriage. This imbalance is insulting to the Christian couple. Do they not need as much preparation to be a visible sign of God's love and holiness?

From a pastoral perspective, I encourage priests to offer couples preparing for marriage an opportunity to evaluate each other's generosity by inviting them to feed the poor...together. This is not meant to be a hoop to jump through, but a personal test of generosity and charity, which are essential virtues they need to share with each other if they hope to make their marriage last. Such an experience would certainly give them a perspective on what it takes to show compassion and love. The opportunity to feed the poor would reroot them in a theological perspective of food by showing how the poor rely on the goodness of God and his Church to make it to the next day. It also gives couples a chance to do an activity of charity together—and in a sense, feed each other with the confidence of developing the skill of providing for each other. It will make them aware of the deeper meaning of their vows to be faithful in good times and bad, in sickness and health, and for richer or poorer. In other words, they will learn ways to love each other when they are *feasting, fasting,* or *starving.* It will deepen the meaning of love for them, as well as humble them and provide them with the chance to see Jesus in the poor, broken, and lonely. The couple will learn how to love those who cannot pay them back. It will increase their love for other people, as the body of Christ, in sickness, poverty, and in their last dying days. These are the vows of marriage that couples must be taught; these are the lessons that the seminarian preparing for priesthood must understand. Together, as the priest and married couples work on the frontlines of this food fight, they will learn to love as Jesus loves, proven by their service to feed the poor.

The Church's social teaching gives a clear mandate to care for the body of Christ by feeding its members—not as a separate experience, but as someone in solidarity. We all have something in common, and feeding each other brings that commonality into reality through a theological perspective of communion and a theology of food. Feeding the poor, eating with and feeding the foreigner, and making sure the well-fed are also spiritually nourished is a means to get the world back on the right path toward salvation.

Following God's diet and obeying his recipe for feeding the poor helps the believer to become more selfless and less selfish.

By learning more about the theological approach to the social teachings of the Catholic Church, God's children become leaders and makers of culture. These teachings bring nations together as one family, feasting at the table of our human experience and learning to love each other—despite our differences—as members of the body of Christ.

The act of feeding the poor expands our understanding of what Jesus meant when he said, "As you did it to one of the least of these my brethren, you did it to me" (Matthew 25:40). As the men and women who have become saints by feeding the poor realized, the very act of feeding others provided nourishment and satisfaction to their own hungry souls. Doing God's will provided them with the spiritual food that fed Christ (see John 4:32 and Matthew 6:25) that corrects and reregulates our flawed diet. Feeding others fits us back into God's plan for saving humanity. The act of caring for those who hunger—for food, faith, friendship, and family—links our human history and propels the body of Christ into the next generation.

SOMETHING TO CHEW ON

Feeding the poor is both a gift and a skill that needs to be developed by the food provider. At most parishes in the United States, parishioners can offer their assistance by providing feeding centers with casseroles, made at home and then delivered to the feeding center. This gesture is a great act of charity, but it's only a partial solution to the problem of poverty. Consider other problems connected to poverty, such as loneliness and depression. It's good and noble to provide food for the homeless and hungry, but it's something else to actually eat with them.

You might consider the following personal experiment in compassion. Visit an actual feeding center or soup kitchen and eat the food they provide. Wait in line, get your tray, find a place to sit, and eat. Try conversing with those around you and consider what could make this experience a moment of grace.

Another common issue is the poor nutritional quality of the food available to the poor. Consider creating a healthier option for feeding the poor, and share this recipe with your local church or feeding center.

Practical Theology for the Dinner Table

1. Are you more inclined to a life of spiritual growth, or are you more active in social justice?

2. In your opinion, what is the most challenging thing about feeding the poor?

3. How do the poor reflect the person of Jesus?

4. Does the grandeur of the Church somehow obscure its mission to be in solidarity with the poor? How do you describe and effectively explain this relationship of the Church with its work to save the poor?

5. If you could create a feeding program for the poor, what would it look like?

CHAPTER SEVEN

The Personal Diet Plan for the Daily Bread

Behold, I stand at the door and knock; if anyone hears my voice and opens the door, I will come in to him and eat with him, and he with me. (Revelation 3:20)

$\mathcal{S}$alvation history is both a universal and personal phenomena. God's desire is to save all of humanity, no matter what religion, race, or creed. God desires all people to be part of the eternal wedding banquet in heaven. A theology of food in the Judeo-Christian perspective provides a fatherly relationship between God and his people. The Church, serving the sacramental role as mother has the same objective: to bring everyone into the heavenly kingdom and feast on the Lamb of God. This is truly a universal approach to humanity.

BOTH A UNIVERSAL AND PERSONAL CALL

How God manifests this universal call to holiness, however, is through each individual's personal response and the relationship shared with each member of his human family. While God loves all people, he loves each person as if that person was the only one on this earth! God's approach to universal salvation is to save each person individually. God sees us personally and individually, and he knows how we will relate to all other peoples and situations globally and eternally. While we are limited by our lack of full consciousness as well as our inherited personal sinful state, we become more a part of God's plan when we enter into the fullest meaning of communion with God and each other. That saving realization comes about when we understand the significance of the Eucharist—when we see it as food for the body, mind, and soul, food that unites us to God and with each other.

The discussion of how food affects our salvation often means engaging a personal diet in order to develop a better sense of self-awareness in terms of what we are putting into our body, mind, and soul. At the same time, each person needs to see how their desire to follow a diet—a personal diet or a theological diet—has more than just personal ramifications. Just as God sees the universal and the personal at the same time, one's individual diet affects both the person and the universe as well. Each person is part of the bigger picture. Furthermore, every life—including lives still being fed from the mother's womb—is worth being saved for eternity because each person has a very necessary part to play in the ultimate salvation of human history.

The Ten Commandments of Personal Dieting

To approach this very big topic, I'd like to offer ten perspectives on personal dieting as it affects salvation history. These commandments are much more than saying "no" to something.

Rather, each one is an invitation to say "yes" to the goodness of God who wants to feed us. When we truly recognize the Hand that feeds us, we can discern other ways to keep the rest of the diet plan.

1. Deepen your understanding of the virtue of moderation.
2. Eat with humility whatever is set before you.
3. Carry the personal cross of your own dietary struggles with dignity.
4. Avoid the temptation to turn a human diet plan into an organized religion.
5. Engage in intentional eating that avoids vanity.
6. Avoid the sins of waste, gluttony, and an immature appetite.
7. Don't engage in scrupulous worry about food.
8. Eat regularly.
9. Pray before every meal.
10. Celebrate each and every bite of food.

These ten perspectives are certainly not meant to be a complete set of rules for a perfect spiritual and physical diet plan. These are simply perspectives that can have an effect on us individually, communally, theological, spiritually, psychologically, and biologically. These considerations for a personal diet can help us see how we fit into the overall plan for salvation. They can help us recognize a bigger plan of being healthy ourselves, thus becoming a more active part in God's saving plan. Let's take a deeper look at each one.

1. Deepen your understanding of the virtue of moderation.

Moderation describes the best attitude and actions of a person who seeks to be healthy in body, mind, and spirit. Moderation is not a cop out, a form of suppression, or living a life without zeal as some may suspect. Moderation also doesn't mean a relativistic attitude without direction. Moderation is not being on the fence. Instead, moderation means that we are able to walk on it without falling off! It implies having a balanced perspective when it comes to life in general. Along with justice, wisdom, and courage, moderation is one of the four cardinal virtues that make a person a saint—the healthiest of all Christians. You can't get any healthier than a saint, someone living forever in heaven!

From a food and faith perspective, moderation implies a deeper investigation of what being a balanced person really means, or eating a balanced diet. Balance implies variety, not just eating the same thing every day, for instance—no matter how healthy that something may be. Variety challenges monotony and boredom and stretches a person's experience beyond the typical and average. Balance requires an open-minded approach to life rather than living a myopic life with blinders that block the view of the bigger picture. At the same time, balance does not mean an excessive use of freedom, doing anything and everything for the sake of balance. We certainly should *not* eat certain things that are harmful. A balanced person knows the difference, while an imbalanced person is not able to discern when they are being too restrictive or too liberal in their approach to life.

Because a person seeking to live a balanced life can be tempted by an overload of information or experiences (which creates an imbalance), balance and moderation require a strong center of gravity. Think of a tree that stays rooted and upright even in the midst of a storm that blows high winds from every direction. Or a tightrope walker who somehow remains rooted on the thin rope, centering and not overcompensating with tendencies or temptations to move in either direction (left or right). Balance, referred to as a "center of gravity," means being rooted in something—or someone.

If we understand being balanced as being rooted in God, moderation in dieting means that what one eats or doesn't eat doesn't determine one's entire existence. Each bite is only part of the bigger picture of the personally balanced diet plan. This rootedness in the divine reminds us that God's initial desire was to feed us everything and anything—except for the forbidden fruit. When we abused God's gift, we lost the balance in our relationship with God.

A theological perspective of food seeks to bring back moderation to a world that is so imbalanced—evidenced by extreme weight gains, extreme weight loss programs, rigid diet plans, and a growing suspicion of food in general. Consider the number of studies that come out each year that frighten people into eating more of this or eating and drinking less of that. At one point, drinking lots of water was healthy; now, it's frowned upon because it bloats and leads to water weight and doesn't create hunger for good foods. Where do we find balance and moderation in the midst of the blowing winds of the day? In God! Let God be the one to feed you and you will see that no diet plan is better than moderation—a true understanding of balance.

2. Eat with humility whatever is set before you.

Humility is connected to balance and moderation. I've had the personal experience of eating with the rich and powerful, as well as the poor and ongoing hungry. And in every case, I can manifest either humility or a lack of it when it comes to food. Jesus spoke of a humble attitude when he reminded his disciples to "eat what is set before you" (Luke 10:8). Especially for the rich, some foods may never be up to their standards. With the plethora of cooking show competitions, though, we can all be rather critical of the food set before us.

The virtue of humility is necessary as it relates to our diet plan. It reminds us that in certain situations we have to just shut up and be grateful for the food we are about to receive, even if we don't want it. Humility in eating makes us more child-like, dependent on others who feed us, and at times, not having a complete say in what we put into our system. I experience this quite often when traveling or at conferences. I could easily become a food critic (and I actually am for a local newspaper), but the virtue of humility reminds me not to be a jerk in the process. It reminds me to be grateful for every bite, being aware that there are starving children in the world who would die (and are dying) to eat what is set before me. If asked in my professional work to critique a meal or a restaurant, I want my motivation to be constructive, not destructive.

Humility in eating also reminds us that food is ultimately just food. While there is status to eating at certain restaurants or ingesting certain foods, it all winds up in the commode! The only exception to this is the spiritual food that remains in the soul as a nutrient that builds up over time and leads us to eternity. This humble approach to eating also reminds us that we will eventually become food ourselves, eaten up by the corrosion that comes with death.

Eating humbly, however, doesn't mean eating bad food for the sake of acting poor! In fact, it can be quite the opposite. Sometimes processed food and fast food is much more expensive than eating healthily. Eating humbly is more of an *attitude* to guide our eating habits. It speaks about the *character* of the diner rather than evaluating what is eaten. For example, some "poor people food" is actually some of the most delicious. If plated properly, a simple taco becomes an expensive entrée. There are simple but delicious Italian pastas, Asian street foods, or inexpensive Mexican tortillas filled with deeply flavored offal. Put in the hands of a masterful and creative chef, these humble foods often become signature dishes—which then leads to a haughty approach to cuisine.

Humility helps us follow God's diet plan well because it helps us remember that eating rich or poor foods will not get us to heaven. Eating the humble food of the Eucharist with a humble heart, however, fulfills the goal of salvation for that faithful dieter.

3. Carry the personal cross of your own dietary struggles with dignity.

Connected to humility is the challenge of the cross for those who suffer with dietary health issues. We all have some dietary restrictions. They may be dairy, nuts, a particular vegetable, or cholesterol. No one can eat just anything without having some kind of a struggle. The alarming (and rising) statistics of those with food allergies and even children diagnosed with eating disorders should make us pause as a nation and ask why. There are those who must now eat a particular type of Communion host. Some cannot partake in a sip of the Precious Blood in the form of wine. Many airlines have stopped serving peanuts due to extreme allergies, and some babies can hardly tolerate their own mothers' breast milk. While those with food allergies can learn to cope with difficult dietary concerns, it still creates a tension and makes them feel as if they cannot fully participate in a party or event. As the "cooking priest," I sometimes have to prepare special meals for people with extreme allergies or health concerns. I'm just grateful they tell me beforehand. And those with food issues experience a natural humility because they always have to make it known that they have certain eating issues. This is truly a cross that they carry, along with their care-givers—especially parents.

How does this fit the model of God's saving grace as it relates to our personal diet? It highlights the uniqueness of each person. But it also shows how these allergies and health issues have come about because of the unhealthy diet we inherited from past generations. Most of the medical sciences confirm that allergies come from multiple sources. We are sometimes born with these genetic defects; others are acquired. In many cases, the dietary issues are a combination of these two factors—nature and nurture. It shows the complexity of our human relationships as well as the human body created by God. Dietary issues humbly remind us that our own biology requires attention in order to live a balanced and healthy life.

At the same time, we are reminded that our diets *today* will affect the diets and health of future generations. And our current diet certainly affects other people, whose health concerns should not make them feel separated from the rest of society. Those with dietary concerns must still be an active part of life. It takes great humility and a strong character to make sure diet issues do not restrict life and limit one's ability to engage the world. Too often we see people who naturally exclude themselves from parties, dinners, or other food gatherings because of health issues. While caution is needed, a more important need is to make sure they do not go without nourishing their souls with the good relationships that come through food!

4. Avoid the temptation to turn a human diet plan into an organized religion.

There is a caution for those who impose strict, almost rigid, personal diets or personal preferences. It's one thing to impose a strict diet if you have a health-related issue. It's another thing to be so zealous about your personal dietary preferences. Just as there are religious zealots and hypocrites, there are those who become "menu zealots" or "food dictators." These people make it unnaturally difficult for everyone else to enjoy a gathering. They might be on such a health kick that they snub their nose at particular celebration food, or they develop such an adherence to a particular diet that they create extra work for the hosts and discomfort among the guests as they (by choice) single themselves out based on their "superior" or "enlightened" food knowledge. It's easy to see how people like this can drag others down. Humility and moderation can help these food relationship situations by remembering the New Testament's understanding of food: All is kosher and good because God made it so (see Acts 10:34–43). What we do with food can render it less nutritious or less flavorful, unhealthy or harmful, but in and of itself, food is food.

People on strict diets ought to be attentive to how a more theological approach to food can help them to be more relational about food and less judgmental. Food is supposed to bring people together; however, there are some who can let personal diets strain relationships by their rigid approach to food.

Some people become so attached to a food movement that they actually treat it like a religious experience. Militant vegans, those who only eat organic food, and even those who swear by certain brands of food need to be careful not to turn food into an end rather than realizing that it is only a *means* to an *end*. Food's real end is helping people to live. A spiritual end may be strengthening relationships, being grateful, and celebrating life!

A good litmus test is to think about whether we would be comfortable eating in certain environments and with different people. I suspect there is a little resistance to this in each of us. Our job is to break that segregation and to overcome the destructive tendencies that draw us away from God's plan for us regarding food and faithful relationships. When we, God willing, get to heaven, there will be all types of food from the

Father's table. Heaven is a place where our perfected natures will just say, "Thank you, God!" and then dig right into the feast without fear and with great faith.

5. Engage in intentional eating that avoids vanity.

Dieters face another struggle, as well as a temptation toward vanity. Here the food and faith connection is quite evident. Dieters endure the difficult course of culinary sacrifices for many reasons. Living a healthy life is a good thing. However, dieting in order to make oneself look attractive can create spiritual problems, even if one is healthier physically. Too many commercials entice people to lose weight in order to improve their appeal. A healthy body is more sexually pleasing, which then can make a person more vain and affect his or her relationship with God.

A theological approach to food can help the dieter put a healthier life into perspective—that watching one's diet makes the body a more suitable temple for the Holy Spirit. Without a theological perspective on food, a dieter can simply strive to make their body a vessel to be admired by others. Such a person is easily tempted to become vain, arrogant, and lustful.

Before you go on a diet, you should check your motivation and intention for losing weight. It may even be helpful to pray that God sustains your efforts in living a more healthy life. Losing weight and being healthier is a blessing from God. Unfortunately, many people become a bit narcissistic after weight loss, giving glory to themselves rather than to God who called them to a healthy lifestyle in the first place.

6. Avoid the sins of waste, gluttony, and an immature appetite.
We should also avoid the sins of waste and gluttony, as well as indulging in an immature appetite. Intentionally wasting food or letting food spoil due to negligence or overbuying is a sin; God did not create anything useless or unhelpful. With God, nothing goes to waste. By not being careful to avoid waste we demonstrate a lack of gratitude, similar to the way a child plays with an expensive toy only once and loses interest in it. The parents who sacrificed to purchase that toy would feel humanly what God experiences morally: disappointment and even a sense of rejection. Note that the sin of waste is not to be confused with an inability to consume everything on your plate because it would make you sick if you ate any more. However, wastefulness is still present in those who serve an overabundance of food, tempting others to either commit the sin of gluttony or overfeeding them to the point of making them ill. It's important to recognize the personal and communal nature of the food and faith relationship.

Gluttony, the inordinate desire of eating and drinking, turns us into irrational beings, making our bellies our gods (see Philippians 3:19) and not accepting our finite ability to take in only so much food or drink. Eating and drinking to excess not only hurts us biologically, it also has spiritual ramifications. It destroys the virtues of temperance and moderation, and it leads to a life of extremes. Besides being gross, it turns us into selfish, weak-willed, undisciplined individuals. In effect, we become slobs, unable to control our appetites and bringing disgrace to refined dining experiences by gorging like irrational animals.

Gluttony is a sin that affects us personally, and it also has an impact on our relationship with God. Gluttony is the opposite of the example of Jesus, who lived a life of temperance and equanimity. By defeating the devil's temptation in the desert, Jesus taught us that we must become masters of our bodies—not allow our bodies to master us! Gluttony easily leads to personal selfishness, a type of hoarding, and a possible retaliation when the disordered appetite is not satisfied. It is a deadly sin, which this modern world, with its insistence on instant gratification, commits more frequently than we're willing to admit.

Another sin (or at least a vice) directly related to food and faith occurs when a person denies themselves opportunities to develop a mature understanding of food. This sin keeps a grown person unappreciative of the finer things in life. While some may say they want to live more "simple" lives, they could actually be sinning by turning themselves into simpletons. They choose not to try new things, instead choosing to eat only the familiar. St. Paul, in his letter to the young St. Timothy, cautioned him to not just drink water, but to drink a little wine for the sake of maturity and health (see 1 Timothy 5:23). St. Paul told the believers at Corinth that they couldn't handle the substance of the truth because they were too immature and used to eating only baby food (1 Corinthians 3:1–2). Some people are so immature that they are satisfied with junk food for the rest of their lives. Their diets have not matured since childhood, and neither have their experiences of formation in the culture and the spiritual life. By not appreciating the finer things in life, they deny themselves the opportunity to grow up. Eating only foods they are familiar with can lead to living a very myopic life—a rigid approach and a fear of stepping outside one's comfort zone.

This close-minded approach to life can lead to being judgmental and critical simply by not being able to appreciate other cultures or traditions. This often manifests itself through having a very narrow diet. On a practical level, by not eating more adult foods, people limit their social constructs and relationships, remain involved only in immature relationships, and this keeps them in a sophomoric frame of mind even as adults. An immature palate turns away the multiple gifts God wants to provide. It rejects different formational experiences that can help shape one's view of the world and the role one plays in it, including the role one plays in salvation history.

7. Don't engage in scrupulous worry about food.

A worry that God won't provide for us doesn't just relate to the spiritual life; it also relates to the culinary world. Many people truly believe they will starve to death. Obviously, in some countries, this might be the case. Yet, in the modern world, there will always be an opportunity to get food supplies to other countries and peoples in need. It just requires humility, patience, and trust, so as not to lose the dignity that turns people into scavengers.

We have all seen instances of this unwarranted fear when a storm comes—even a simple snowstorm—and people overreact by emptying grocery store shelves, or begin hoarding for some impending disaster. There is a difference between preparing for a rainy day and those who are consumed by worry, obsessing about the idea that somehow they will not have enough to eat.

Again, while in some countries that may be true, the plethora of food in our own cabinets shows that our fears of starvation are irrational.

Worry, as well as a hyper form of obsession (understood spiritually as "scrupulosity"), can be harmful to a person's mind, relationships, and their understanding of God's saving action. This imbalanced worry and obsessive fear is a temptation to mistrust God's providence. This is what motivates people to rob, steal, cheat, or lie in order to survive. It's a temptation the devil uses to make us believe that God doesn't hear our cries and or won't share his blessings with us. Scrupulous worrying leads to hopelessness, an obvious temptation to not believe God's saving actions in the past. That's why God required the Jewish people to commemorate the feast days as a reminder that he has continued to feed his people—and always will!

This fear can be healed with a more trusting faith, a discipline to fast on certain days, charity and generosity with others, and the humility to ask for help when necessary. Worrying about food affects us—our bodies, our souls, and our minds. Think about how the fear of starvation for the Jewish people prompted God's incredible actions through Moses in the desert for forty years. We may struggle for forty hours or even forty days. But the Jews' forty *years* in the wilderness help us remember that God always provided.

8. Eat intentionally.

This perspective is really more of a hint for those who are trying to improve their culinary and spiritual diet plan. The advice to eat multiple small meals throughout the day, also known as *intentional eating*, reduces hunger throughout the day. In many cultures, including my own Filipino tradition, it's customary to eat about five small meals each day. Regular, intentional eating gives a healthy perspective to the physical and spiritual life. Instead of trying to satisfy one's hunger all at one time, intentional eating disciplines one's body, mind, and spirit to be nourished with smaller but regular portions. This is ultimately healthier because it trains the stomach and the appetite to be satisfied—as opposed to the roller-coaster approach to dieting that many people endure.

People who don't eat with intention tend to starve themselves, eating only when they are really hungry. They attempt to fill their day with busyness to occupy their desire for a meal. Keeping busy helps them to forget they are getting hungry. When they finally have time to remember that they are human, they feel intense hunger pangs and are tempted to gorge. Such an approach creates confusion for one's body and mind. Starving and gorging shrinks and expands the stomach, never giving this vital organ the strength and stability that comes from intentionally eating regular and smaller portions.

Intentional eating also affects one's spirit. We become healthier by feeding our souls and minds regularly. Small bites of truth sprinkled throughout the day can actually be more helpful for a person than attempting an overdose of spirituality all at once. God commanded a regular Sabbath—an intentional day of rest for believers to feast on God's goodness. Some of us practice our faith irregularly and unhealthily, celebrating with God's family once or twice a year, or only occasionally without regularity. Some go to church only when there is a problem. They pray sporadically when they have time. This attitude and approach is no different from those who eat irregularly. Neither creates stability, and both tempt a person to live an extreme life—feast or famine.

9. Pray before every meal.

This one might sound like a shameless plug for my movement, Grace Before Meals (www.gracebeforemeals.com), but it's actually something I've found to be incredibly helpful to many people. By taking time to pray before eating—not just the typical glib, monotonous prayer often said, but an honest, sincere prayer— actually has an effect on the mind and soul of the diner. From a physical perspective, it slows us down and gives us the opportunity to be more reflective, grateful, and humble. A prayer before a meal establishes a sacramental moment; we are reminded that God is present because we have invited him to our table with that sincere prayer. And if we recognize that God is the guest at our table, wouldn't we eat more maturely, more responsibly, less selfishly, and more healthfully? We would have an awareness that the One who made the body cares about what goes into it.

10. Celebrate each and every bite of food.

Saying grace before meals leads to my last suggestion: Truly celebrate each meal! Think of the type of Thanksgiving cele- bration, as the family gathers around an intentionally beautiful meal prepared with love. When the time comes to bless the food, a power comes over each member. Those paying attention and really trying to enter into the prayer recognize their humble historical roots, the struggles of our country's forefathers who sacrificed their lives in order for us to have freedom. They humbly recall how many people go without family, food, faith, and friendship. This beautiful experience does not have to be limited to one day a year; it can be your experience each time you eat.

Celebrating food reminds us that each bite is a gift from God. It fosters an attitude of humility and gratitude, and also joy and hope. The opposite of celebration is drudgery, pain, and boredom. Too many of us are tempted to live like this. We easily forget that a meal is a gift to be celebrated. The idea of celebrating each meal, no matter how simple it may be, requires discipline. A quote from Voltaire sums it up well: "Nothing would be more tiresome than eating and drinking if God had not made them a pleasure as well as necessity."[4]

Life gives each of us enough challenges, struggles, and pain. When we look at salvation history, the only thing that really helped people to overcome was *celebrating life*. Even challenges can be faced with joy when we take the initiative to live life more fully.

Psalm 126:5 says, "May those who sow in tears reap with shouts of joy!" This verse validates the call to celebrate each bite. How did these Old Testament harvesters get through the backbreaking efforts of sowing seed? They first of all remembered that hard work produces fruit, and they also remembered that a great celebration always follows the harvest. If we don't remember to celebrate, it may be because we're not working hard enough, or perhaps we have forgotten to be grateful for the gift of the fruits of our labor. Some people work to live, while others live to work. However, we need a balance of both these attitudes to have a healthy diet for our body, mind, and soul.

The celebration at the end of a difficult day, or taking time throughout the day to pause and take a much-needed rest from our efforts works with the biological need to satisfy hunger. We ought to celebrate each time we find an opportunity to satisfy our hunger. When we eat a simple granola bar, get a quick shot of espresso, have a power lunch, and especially when we have a chance to share a quiet dinner with a special friend or loved one, each bite sustains us through the weariness of life's many crosses, and for that we ought to be grateful. An intentional attitude to celebrate each meal creates in us the humility of a child who stops crying when his mother nurses him. It brings us joy when the simple ingredients of flour, eggs, and sugar are baked into a festive birthday cake. Celebration comes when we bring a casserole to the local soup kitchen and watch the faces of those who would not otherwise eat if it were not for the kindness of these food heroes.

Celebrating each bite reminds me of a unique call I received to give last rites to an older gentleman, a pillar in the community and a faithful, loving father who was in his last moments of life. Normally, I would bring Communion to give as viaticum, the last sacred bite that would accompany him in his journey to heaven. However, in this case I was told the patient could not take anything orally. So, I came with just my oils, holy water, stole, prayer book, and my priestly faith to assist this dying man.

Surrounded by his loving family, teary-eyed but hopeful, we prayed together. Along with the ritual, we prayed in thanksgiving and celebration of this man's life, now in its final moments. At the end of the prayer, this man looked up at a presence no one else could see. He stretched out his feeble arms and hands the way someone ready to receive Communion at Mass would. He clearly mouthed the word "Amen" and cupped something in his hands. To our wonder and amazement, he put his hands to his mouth and chewed. A look of serenity came over him. He closed his eyes and rested. Later that day, the man died.

What did he have in his hands? Why did he visibly mouth the word "Amen"? What did he eat that gave him such rest and peace? Could that bite-sized mysterious morsel have been the viaticum—the supernatural and super-substantial food that looks like bread but possesses invisible power?

I think that when we approach food with a sense of awe and reverence as someone eating their last bite—or as a Last Supper—we approach this gift with a deeper sense of our higher calling.

BEARING THE GOOD FRUIT OF SALVATION HISTORY

We've seen throughout this book how food has an impact on more than just our bodies. When we humbly consider this gift, we become aware of how food affects body, mind, and soul. The food we share with others powerfully affects not just us; it can also impact the world.

These insights, however, would remain incomplete if we did not consider the One who provides food for us in the first place. For this reason, a developing theology of food ought to help us reflect on how each bite—and especially the one bite of the blessed fruit of Mary's womb that hangs from the Tree of Life—corrects the venom of the forbidden fruit and gets us back on track to God's original intentions for the human race. This one bite helps us to experience salvation history bearing fruit in our own lives. If we bear good fruit in this life, this must be shared with those who hunger for the cup of life and the bread of eternal salvation.

The eternal food fight will continue in the soul of each person who hungers for God. Thank God the victory has been given to us—in our hands, in our mouths, and on our tongues. One bite of this victorious food sustains us daily, strengthens our weariness, and brings us to everlasting life —the goal of all of salvation history.

SOMETHING TO CHEW ON

Diet plans are not easy for a family. However, it can be even more difficult for a single person; it can become very expensive to purchase groceries for one person. Fresh ingredients are often packaged in bulk, making it easy to waste food. Buying only enough for one can become so expensive that singles are tempted to purchase less healthy (but more convenient) options such as frozen entrees or fast food. While it takes an organized person to create menus for an entire family, it takes that same skill for a single person to purchase properly so that little goes to waste. Over-purchasing and overeating creates much unhealthiness in our modern world. It's a problem that affects most single people, including our overweight clergy, those who are widowed, divorced, or empty-nesters.

As part of a plan to organize your diet, it helps to organize your purchases so you can get as much out of one product as possible. For example, take the purchase of a whole chicken. Families and single diners are prone to purchasing chicken parts, yet it is more economical to buy a whole chicken, learn how to butcher and store it properly, and master a few recipes using different parts of the chicken. This gives diners a variety of flavors with less cost and less waste.

For example, the day you purchase a whole chicken, immediately butcher the chicken, properly storing the different parts for different meals throughout the week. One day you can fillet the chicken breasts and create multiple dishes such as chicken parmesan or chicken Francais. Using the wings, you can make a great snack of hot wings. The legs can be cooked and pulled apart for a flavorful sandwich. The thighs, when deboned, are great for stuffing and wrapping with a slice of bacon. Save the bones and boil them in water with some onions, carrots, and celery for a homemade stock for soups or deglazing pan-prepared foods.

A healthy diet requires organization, education, inspiration, and discipline. While it's easier to just purchase chicken parts for a particular meal, it's more expensive and ultimately less creative—that is, boring!

People waste a lot of their food purchases or prepare uninspired meals because they lack proper instruction. Education aids a balanced diet—for a family or a single person. A theology of food encourages all of God's children to learn more about the food they eat by taking a nutrition class or a course on the basics of a different cultural cuisine.

I've taught some of these skills to seminarians to help them eat more healthily as future priests. They are now more mature and prepared to take care of themselves in their own rectory. In teaching them, I tried to make sure that my students experienced a variety of flavors, explored different cultures, and had fun by inviting different friends over for a meal or starting a lunch club with friends and coworkers.

The best personal diets and the healthiest people enjoy variety, inspiration, fun, and—above all—faithful observation of God's diet plan.

PRACTICAL THEOLOGY FOR THE DINNER TABLE

1. What is the most successful diet that you've been on?
2. When do you feel healthiest—body, mind, and spirit?
3. What is your favorite celebration food, and why?
4. How can diets be helpful or hurtful?
5. If heaven is really a banquet, what foods and what guests would you want to be there, and why? How can you bring a hint of that celebration as a foretaste of heaven to your table now?

1. Mary is traditionally called the Mirror of Justice as part of the Litany of Loreto, based on 1 Corinthians 13:12. See Mirror of Justice, the Mary Page, http://campus.udayton.edu/mary/prayers/speculumjustitiae.html.

2. Quoted at http://www.ourcatholicprayers.com/aquinas-before-communion.html.

3. Note the new English translation of the words used by the priest in the Institution of the Eucharist. Previously, the priest said over the chalice, "It will be shed for you and for *all*." Now it says, "for you and the *many*." This creates a unique teaching that not all, but many will be saved. Respecting the gift of free choice, many will choose to share in this meal, but not all.

4. Quoted at http://thinkexist.com/quotation/nothing_would_be_more_tiresome_than_eating_and/345268.html.

About the Author

Father Leo Patalinghug is a Roman Catholic priest who holds a pontifical theological degree in Mariology. He is also an international TV show host, radio host, and founder of the international movement Grace Before Meals. He is a popular speaker and the author of *Grace Before Meals* and *Spicing Up Married Life.*